MIND AND BODY

TRANSFORMATION

The Cheat Code To Unlocking

Your Greatest Potential

Dr. Robert L. Evans, III

Copyright © 2025 by Dr. Robert Evans, III
All rights reserved.

No part of this publication may be reproduced, distributed, or transmitted in any form or by any means, including photocopying, recording, or other electronic or mechanical methods, without the prior written permission of the publisher, except in the case of brief quotations embodied in critical reviews and certain other noncommercial uses permitted by copyright law. For permission requests, write to the publisher, addressed "Attention: Permissions Coordinator," to the email: drevans@empowertoday.net.

This publication is designed to provide accurate and authoritative information in regard to the subject matter covered. While the publisher and author have used their best efforts in preparing this book, they make no representations or warranties with respect to the accuracy or completeness of the contents of this book and specifically disclaim any implied warranties of merchantability or fitness for a particular purpose. No warranty may be created or extended by sales representatives or written sales materials. The advice and strategies contained herein may not be suitable for your situation. You should consult with a professional when appropriate. Neither the publisher nor the author shall be liable for any loss of profit or any other commercial damages, including but not limited to special, incidental, consequential, personal, or other damages.

First Printing, 2025

Hardback ISBN: 978-1-7372211-5-9

Paperback ISBN: 978-1-7372211-6-6

E-Book ISBN: 979-8-9928732-0-7

Printed in the United States of America

Contents

Foreword xi

Preface xv

   Perception 2

   The Mind 10

STAGE ONE Why? 22

   True Desire 23

   Your "Why" Must Be Greater 25

   The Divine in You 28

STAGE TWO Intentionality 31

   Self-Awareness 33

   Desire 38

   Intentionality Haters 43

      Feelings 43

      Strategy: Put a Pin in the Emotion, Assess, Create (PAC)! .. 45

      Distorted Thinking 46

Strategy: Assess, Seek, and Keep It Moving (ASK)!............47

STAGE THREE Mind & Body Alignment (MBA) 51

    Consistency..65
        Structure..65
        Cockiness...71
        Strategy: Thought Management! 74

STAGE FOUR Inqubo..78

    Emotions..82
        Targeting Emotions 84
        Core Beliefs..87
    Vagus Nerve..90
    Vagal Tone..95

Infinity Stone #1 100

Infinity Stone #2 107

Infinity Stone #3 115

    Positive Self-Affirmations.....................................119
    Negative Self-Threats...120

Infinity Stone #4 123

Infinity Stone #5 129

    Acute Stress Response (Fight or Flight) 141
        Cross-Stressor Adaptation Hypotheses 150
        Transformation Simulation 161
        Crisis Thinking 163

The Mind & Body Cheat Code (MBCC) 167

        Cheat Code/My Daily Routine 171

Infinity Stone #6 177

Dr. E's Research Study 190

Acknowledgments 205

About the Author 209

References 211

Dedication

Chess, much the same as life, is a game of causality. Each move directly influences not only your next move but every possible move on the board. Comparatively, in life, every decision we make not only cascades into the next one but also results in a corollary, forever imprinting the lives of those touched by that decision. As a psychotherapist, I assist my clients with understanding and appreciating how their thinking and behavior paint the canvas of their lives so that they can make the best decisions, resulting in desired outcomes. In many instances, to achieve their goals, my clients must heal from past trauma, develop a positive self-image, learn to trust themselves, navigate fractured relationships, master their emotions, and build self-confidence.

In my mission to provide them with the most efficacious and cutting-edge therapeutic tools, I developed what I initially referred to as "The Emotional Cheat Code". That was before I realized how this tool transcends emotions and covers every aspect of self-development imaginable. So, the strategy was given a more fitting title. This book illustrates the now dubbed Mind & Body Cheat Code (MBCC), which is the primary tool I use in therapy; thus, this book is dedicated to some of the most insightful, intelligent, caring, hardworking, courageous, determined, and hilarious people I know... my clients. My clients have held a flashlight along my journey of self-discovery as a clinician and, ultimately, the quest to discover the best version of myself thus far, and for that, I am eternally grateful. Please accept my sincere gratitude for entrusting in me your most intimate thoughts, your greatest fears, your pain, your shame, and your love. I truly value my calling and do my best to lead by example both in and outside of my office. So, in honor of my clients, I am gifting you with this magical approach to self-emergence that will only work if you work it! As you will see, it will not be an easy road, but then, what on earth worth anything ever is? The greatest joy I have ever experienced in my career is a breakthrough, and the MBCC can be credited for countless groundbreaking moments. I can only pray it does the same for you!

Foreword

In life, no matter who you are, where you come from, or how much money you have, you will face hard times. As so many of us would say, and as Dr. Evans, aka "Dr. E," quoted in Mind & Body Transformation, "Life be 'lifing'." We will indeed fall! But how will we get back up? My name is Gregory Outlaw Jr. I'm a professional boxer and current WBA NBA Jr. Welterweight and NBA Welterweight Champion of the world with a record of 17-2 (10 KOs). Although I win a lot, I have hit the canvas a few times during my boxing career, and those times could be viewed by some as losses. However, moments like those only count as losses if I quit or don't learn. In my opinion, the 'L" stands for lessons. Lessons that helped build my character.

DR. ROBERT L. EVANS, III

My journey growing up as a young Black man in this country has been very interesting, to say the least. I have fallen short so many times in my life, but I've always gotten up. As I said before, "life be lifing," and since we're all in this together, I don't complain. I especially feel this way about persons of color. In a system that I feel was never designed to protect us, we often need FAITH, mental toughness, and tools like the Mind & Body Cheat Code (MBCC) to prevail and push through. I am truly thankful for a praying mother and praying grandmother who continues to show the power of faith. Faith is the only thing I had to stand 10 toes down on until I met Dr. E, who literally gives us the tools to overcome and unlock our greatest potential in his books *Run to the Pain* and *Mind and Body Transformation.*

I may fall, but I will never stay down! I know my *Why*! I love how the first thing Dr. E. touches on is your "*Why.*" The reason this is Stage I in the book is because this is most important. This sets the tone! Your *Why* is your foundation. As Dr. E. stated in the book, "The first step of the *Why* stage is to search our gut and identify our genuine desire... Your *Why* must be Greater." My *Why* is greater than any obstacle I will face; however, I am human, and there are times when the devil knows how to creep doubt into my mind. The MBCC gives us the tools needed to overcome any challenge the enemy throws against us!

One of the most important tools that Dr. E. has given us in the MBCC is learning how to train/condition the physiological aspect of our body's acute stress response. Dr. E. has given us the tools to overcome anger, stress, trials, and tribulations. He is training us for mental and emotional War. Not to brag, but I've had the privilege of seeing Dr. E. practice/train using the MBCC himself. Being a professional boxer who does "HIIT" training 7 days a week, as well as dealing with life challenges- (road rage lol), the breathing techniques have become essential tools for me to stay patient, happy, stress-free, and confident in and out of the ring.

Today, as I write this foreword for Dr. E's life-changing book, I share words with gratitude and certainty that this book will change your life if you apply the tools given. Practice these tools and methods in times of peace so that when the war comes, you will not panic. You will be fully qualified and equipped. TRAIN! TRAIN! TRAIN! You practice how you play! And don't forget, **Work don't stop... PEOPLE DO!**

- Greg "Sharpshooter" Outlaw, Jr.

Preface

In 2020, amidst the deadliest and most economically crippling biochemical and infectious pandemic of my lifetime, the crucial role of adversity in each of our lives surfaced. I came to understand and embrace the principal goal of affliction, to not only unveil our inadequacies but to usher you and me into the supreme versions of ourselves. Hence, as it pertains to life's adversities, I transitioned quickly from a back-peddle to not just an approach but a *Run to the Pain*.

On 3/21/2020, I began a journey that I have continued relentlessly since that day. On that day, during the COVID-19 epidemic, the governor of Maryland, where I lived, shut down public movement for non-essential workers and allowed it for emergencies only. Businesses where the public would gather for non-essential activities were ordered to cease operations until further notice. It was at that time that I was faced with a decision. I would either accept the reasonable excuse to stop exercising on my usual three-days-per-week schedule, or I would decide to condition myself to step up my game during times of trepidation, chaos, and hardship. You have heard the saying, "When the going gets tough, the tough get going." Well, let's just say I got going!

2/01/25 marked 254 consecutive weeks of exercising, at least Monday through Friday, without exception. It also marked 455 consecutive days of pushups since 11/1/2023 and 409 consecutive days of sit-ups since 12/19/23. I promise you unless I'm currently laid up in a hospital or 6 feet underground, the streak is still going as of the day you are reading this book. The success of this streak has been no fluke and cannot be written off as happenstance. It has been intentional, and it is an unequivocal result of the Mind & Body Cheat Code (MBCC).

To date, the efficacy of the MBCC is based not only on extensive research of its individual elements, but the theory has been expressly informed by autoethnographic research. The MBCC is unique, in that it is comprised of several individually robust fields of study. Consequently, the secret sauce is in the specific combination of these ingredients. Heretofore, outside of using myself as the primary participant, there is no other experimental research that supports the validity of this recipe. Accordingly, I would comport the experiment myself if I had available time. However, since I do not, later in this book I outline how I would administer a research study of the MBCC using participants other than myself. Hopefully, someone with available time and resources will take on the challenge. If you do, I would love to participate in the study as a fellow researcher.

The interesting thing about the MBCC is that I discovered and explored the various elements of the strategy prior to understanding how they all interact with each other and essentially work together to garner self-transformation. It wasn't until I felt the positive results from combining the puzzle pieces that I began to do some digging to see if anyone else discovered this life hack. I was not surprised to see that researchers had already begun to explore combining some of the fields of study. However, I was excited to uncover that there is still so much more space to explore how combining the ingredients, as outlined in this book, can tap into the power of neuroplasticity and essentially give us the agency to manipulate and ultimately change every aspect of who we are. Essentially, the MBCC is the key to getting you "unstuck," which is one of the most common complaints I receive from new clients.

The Mind & Body Cheat Code is a formula, and if the recipe is followed precisely as outlined in this book, you WILL have unlocked and accessed the competence to:

- regulate your emotions
- eliminate anxiety
- eradicate anger
- quash maladaptive behaviors and toxic habits
- improve your physical health
- manage your mental health
- enrich your spiritual health
- reinvent your self-image
- defeat procrastination
- improve self-trust
- increase consistency
- become the best you
- commit to the best you

- recommit to the best you

The discovery of the MBCC happened in stages. Like a pyramid, each stage provided a foundation for the next to build upon. I also observed that not only did each stage flow into the next, but they operated simultaneously when the cheat code was being effectively practiced.

Stage I: Why?

Stage II: Intentionality

Stage III: Mind & Body Alignment

Stage IV: Inqubo

Like a soup or gumbo, while each ingredient maintains its own integrity of flavor, they are essential for the recipe, and all merge together for the combustion of tasteful joy. Again, in 2020, I began this journey, and the learning lessons along the way gave birth to my first book, *Run to the Pain*, in 2021. In that book, I touched on some of the first three stages of the MBCC. Hence, this book is somewhat of a sequel, as it picks up where the first book left off on the road to becoming the best version of self. Therefore, if you have already read *Run to the Pain*, feel free to read this book from Soup to Nuts, permitting some of the information to be a refresher. However, I highly recommend that after you digest the introduction, you do not simply skip to the dessert in stage number four, as there are new therapeutic tools and content in all courses of the meal. With that said, grab your fork and knife, tie on your bib, and Bon Appetit!

"True rewards come from engaging fully with the process, not just the outcome.."

- Jonvoana R. Evans,
*While I Was Waiting on God,
He Was Waiting on Me*

"Just Start"

- Dr. Robert Evans, III

Introduction

Perception

Around the year 1984, at the age of 5 or 6 years old, I remember being in the back seat of my dad's Toyota Tercel when we hit a patch of ice while driving at night. The car started spinning in the middle of the road. Back then, cars had lap belts in the rear, and I think I unbuckled mine or never had it on because I was holding onto the back of the front passenger seat while the car was doing 360° donuts. I remember having the time of my life. It felt like I was on a tea-cup ride at the amusement park, having my head pulling in one direction with my neck and the rest of my body pulling in the other. I remember something that felt like an explosion of warm water surging in my stomach and chest while my hands and arms were doing the best they could to hold on to the front seat of the car. My heart was pounding harder with each oscillation of the Tercel. We were twirling for what felt like a full ride at the park. When the car came to a stop, I remember cheering in the back seat, wanting more. "Again! Again! Again!"

Coincidentally, as you can imagine, my father's experience was on the opposite end of the emotional spectrum. I recall glancing at him during this thrill ride that was in the middle of a city intersection and not controlled by the systems and confines of an amusement park. I saw him vigorously sliding his hands on the wheel in different directions as the car was spinning. Even now, I can think back and see an image of him doing his best to gain control of the car. What I did not know was the sliding of the hands on that wheel, going in the direction of the spinning, along with intermittent pumping of the breaks, was law enforcement training kick'n in! At that time, at 5 or 6 years old, I had no clue about my father's perception of that moment. All I knew was it was fun. A burst of warmth surged in both his stomach and chest. Tightening of his muscles, increased strength, sweat, elevated heart rate, sharpened reflexes, and reaction time. For my father, while that same event did generate similar chemical and physical responses inside, it did not equate to the same experience. The same physiological reactions to the situation registered for me as excitement and simultaneously recorded for my father as fear. At that moment, he was petrified... Perception!

Around 2011, my oldest son was playing youth football for a 12u full-contact team. I enjoyed watching and sometimes participating in his practices. I remember one practice where he was running through a tackle drill with another teammate. He had somewhat of a rivalry with this kid. They both ran hard and when they went against each other, they collided with violence and thunderous impact. For this drill, the teammate carried the football and ran at an angle full speed while my son had to tackle him. One hit after another, you could hear their shoulder pads echoing across the field. Then, CRACK!!!... the dust cleared, and there was my son on the ground screaming in a pitch so loud it could shatter glass. I ran over and asked him what was hurting, and he looked over towards his shoulder and screamed, "My arm!!" ... seconds later, he looked again, and suddenly, he was silent. I asked him, "What happened?" ... His reply was, "I thought my arm was off my body!" I still laugh about that moment to this day. He felt a sharp pain from the collision, and when he looked and saw himself lying on the ground, his mind registered that his arm was disconnected, and he lost it! ... Perception!

In 2023, I took my family on a vacation to Kissimmee Florida. We went to an amusement park, and three of my daughters wanted to get on a "Sky Coaster," which is a swing ride that drops from super high in the air, carrying the weight of the rider(s) into an enormous swinging back and forth. Ryan, aka Ry or Cute Poop, TaRheeyn, aka Rheeny Pop, and Tamir, aka Mir Mir, strapped into a harness and were hoisted into the air 250 feet. Click... Click... Click... A saddle slowly cranked the three of them to the highest point. As they were being lifted into the air, I watched from a rooftop. I could feel my stomach dropping even before they started their dive.

Increased heart rate, muscles tightening, palms sweating, and the sensation of butterflies fighting in their stomachs. They shared the event along with the internal physical reactions to it. Meanwhile, their external physical dispositions were very different. Pop was hyped from the start. She ran over to the harness and was talking trash even before they started their ascent. She was obviously excited. Clapping her hands and pumping her fist. Mir's excitement was less visible. As the oldest, I'm sure she felt like she had to be the mature one in the situation. She appeared to be someone who was simply ready for war. Ry was true to form, handling the situation in a very cerebral way. As an observer, it may appear that she is disengaged or not enjoying herself at times when the reality is she is extremely dialed into the activity and recording every second of it. Her outward excitement was displayed later in the ride. In fact, when they arrived at the pinnacle of the ride, Ry was the one who had to pull the lever for the girls to begin their free-fall from 250 feet in the air. I watched the three of them at the release of the harness as their weight merged with the force of gravity and plunged them towards the earth. Their faces and screams were the looks and sounds of exhilaration. Now, if they were plummeting to the ground without the protection of the harness, what feeling would their looks and sounds represent? ... Perception!

One last quick story on perception before we get into the first stage. One day I was exercising with a weight vest on. As I neared the end of the workout, I felt pain settling in on my shoulders. I remember saying to myself, "Man this is starting to hurt." Then my understanding of perception kicked in and I was reminded of the power of self-affirmations and our internal dialogue. So, I immediately refuted that defeatist statement and said to myself, "No it doesn't! It's light as a feather! Light as a feather! Light as a feather! ... Almost instantly, the pain in my shoulders subsided. It felt miraculous ... Perception!

100% of your reality is your perception of any given moment. Your thoughts are solely responsible for how pleasant or harmful, comfortable, or disagreeable you perceive a situation to be. Prov. 23:7 (KJV) says, "For as he thinketh in his heart, so is he." It is important to understand and completely adopt the concept of perception because as we go into the components of the MBCC, if you do not manage your perspective of each field of study, you will miss its significance, thus devaluing the entire method. For example, if you believe in the benefits of physical activity but do not perceive self-affirmations to be useful, you have already sabotaged the success of the entire strategy, as both physical activity and self-affirmations are key ingredients in the recipe. Additionally, each element of the MBCC is an activity of perception development and manipulation. Moreover, each of the foundational elements of the inqubo stage culminates in a psychological simulation that will only work if one fully embraces the influence of perception over reality. Simply put, the MBCC is a technique in perception control. Control your perception, and you control your reality. With that said, do yourself a favor and approach this method with an open mind, free of apprehensions, preconceived notions, and self-imposed limitations. Anything is possible, and very few truer words have ever been spoken. Just remember, while 100% of your reality is your perception of any given moment, it is never the most informed view of reality. Ergo, always be open to considering the viewpoints of others to develop a well-rounded and comprehensive perspective.

The Mind

Rather than leave you with perception and jump into the main course, I believe it's necessary to double down on the power of thought, which is the primary faculty of the mind, and the mind is the headquarters for perception. Mastery of thought processing is mastery of the mind. As a psychotherapist, I assist people with mind mechanics, better known as executive functions, such as prioritizing, time management, task initiation, and goal persistence. We work through self-dialogue skills, thought management competence, and questions such as, "What should I do next? ... How should I handle this?...and What should I say?" In essence, I guide people through the process of making up their minds.

What is the mind? The mind is the agency that facilitates the operation of our thoughts, feelings, and behaviors: our entire existence. It is the animation of an idea, that is brain activity. The mind is the progeny of a complex network of brain cells at work, receiving information from the internal and external environment, transforming the filtered information into "our experience of ourselves, the world around us, and our relationships with it" (Badcock, P., 2019).

But what makes the mind work? In theory, the body is a self-energy generating and self-sustaining battery. According to Purves et al., the movement of ions across cell membranes, a process called "electric action potential" (Drukarch & Wilhelmus, 2023), is what generates electrical charges in the body that keep our hearts pumping and that sustain the brain and gut's communal relationship. In other words, according to science, our body's internal procedures simply act, pursuing life, without any outside influence. Without getting too philosophical, I believe in science to a certain extent. Science, like theology, can only explain things to a point, and then there is faith, which is the belief in that which is unseen or has no evidence of existence (Hebrews 11:1, KJV). With that said, I'll provide a bit of science and a peek into my theological perspective.

In science class, we learned about the "basic unit of life," the cell (Hatton, Galbraith, Merleau, Miettinen, Smith, & Shander, 2023). It is the "structural and functional unit" of all living organisms, and it is a "model of the whole organism represented in a small unit" (Mostafa, 2021). Depending on the size of a person, the human body is comprised of 17 to 35 trillion cells (Hatton et al., 2023). In 2021, Mostafa posited that there are 215 types of cells with all of them working for our good. Muscle cells, blood cells, skin cells, bone, and stem cells are just a few of the many types of cells determined to equip us with the ability to not just survive but experience an enjoyable quality of life. In this book, I will focus on the cells responsible for generating thoughts and feelings, which are intrinsically the cells of the mind, the nerve cells (Alcohol Health Res World, 1997).

Herculano-Houzel proffered in 2009 that there are about 85 billion nerve cells in the human brain. Nerve cells, or Neurons, are the "key players" in the operation of the nervous system, the body's communication network, conveying information electrically and chemically to essentially control every aspect of the body's functioning (Alcohol Health Res World, 1997). I will dive into aspects of the nervous system later, but for now, let's identify that the central nervous system consists of the brain and spinal cord, and in conjunction with the peripheral nervous system, it is responsible for the transformational outcomes this book will highlight (Newman T, 2023). Mind mechanics such as emotional regulation, self-control, goal-directed persistence, prioritization, flexible thinking, and performance monitoring, along with vagal nerve-influenced behaviors like breathing, heart rate, and hormones, are all governed by the central nervous system. (Diamond A, 2012; Newman T, 2023).

My first introduction to the potential of the mind came during my undergraduate studies at Towson University. I was studying maladaptive behavior and mental health disorders when I learned about dissociative identity disorder (DID), previously known as multiple personality disorder (MPD). Note, in 1986, Putnam et al. studied MPD and defined the different personalities within an individual as an "alter." They further described an alter as a "distinct state of consciousness with a unique personality" (Putnam et al., 1986). In my readings, I acquired some fascinating discoveries about alters that underscored the reach of the mind. For instance, what if I told you that there is a research study of a patient with DID having multiple alters who were misdiagnosed with cortical blindness for over 15 years, and with psychotherapy, several of the alters regained their vision? (Strasburger & Waldvogel, 2015).

What was even more astonishing was research purported by Dr. Bennett Braun in the mid-1980s, speaking of cases where a person diagnosed with MPD had multiple alters with diabetes and needed insulin while other alters did not. Since we know that diabetes results from a lack of insulin production and malfunctioning of the pancreas (Charley, Dinner, Pham, & Vyas, 2023), Braun's research suggested that the pancreas of a patient with MPD would work properly for some alters and fail to work for others. If this is true, this is an exhibition of the mind's boundless capacity. What limit does a mind have when it can cause an alter to experience diabetes and require insulin, while other alters within the same person do not require it? Unfortunately, much of Dr. Braun's research was tarnished due to a scandal he was wrapped up in, which consequently led to the loss of his license to practice psychiatry.

While there are still prevailing questions surrounding his research, more recent studies on diabetes and DID have supported the idea of a dissociative episode being triggered by a lapse in taking prescribed diabetes medications (Ram, Ashoka, & Gowdappa, 2015). While this research is not the same as Braun's, it connotes the belief that perception and behavior are manifestations of the mind's engineering.

This context is being provided to punctuate the dense intricacy of the mind's composition. Basically, for people to make up their minds, it requires a king-sized amount of cooperation amongst the faculties of the brain. However, there is more to the myth of the mind. I say myth loosely because although in the world of science, it is still an enigma, it is very much a reality. A reality that, once understood for its potential, would be intentionally shaped and targeted to achieve specific and desired outcomes. The Cheat Code illustrated in this book will do just that... teach you how to turn your mind into a goal-seeking and achieving rocket. And what about the notion that our consciousness, our mind, and our thoughts are concepts that are just so? As previously mentioned, the electricity in our body is what generates the motion of the impulses and internal mechanisms that make our bodies move, but then the question is, Why? In my research as to what causes this chain of events in our bodies to even start and why, science has no answers. When you ask the question, "Well, what causes the electrical action potential to begin?" It leads you down a rabbit hole of terms such as depolarization, ion movement, channel opening, and positive feedback loops, leading you right back to the same starting point in a circular motion (Purves et al., 2001; Mitrophanov & Groisman, 2008; Wang, X., et al., 2022).

Here is where science taps out, and faith begins. You may be asking, "What is the relevance of a faith discussion?." Well, thanks for asking! I will get into the divine aspect of our "*Why*" in the first stage. However, for now, think about the fact that the strategy in this book is going to teach you how to initiate movement toward your goals, how to become consistent, and how to prioritize yourself. Then, think about the available options to execute these objectives. There is either a scientific explanation that will assist people with motivation, drive, and intentionality, or there is a faith-based rationale. Remember, according to science, the initiatory movement of electrical impulses and physiological processes within our bodies that result in thoughts, feelings, and behaviors just happens because it happens. If this is reality, then there is frankly no purpose for life outside of sheer survival; thus, no reason to strive for self-improvement or to become the best version of ourselves. Conversely, there is simply no way I can exclude the infinite power of faith and its utter gravity on our intentionality. Truly, both science and faith work in concert when it comes to a mind and body transformation. Your mission, should you choose to accept it, is to learn how to channel your faith into an igniter of your physical progression toward your desired outcomes. Fortunately, this book reveals the blueprint to get'er done!

Quick story about the obvious and profound nature of faith and its union, yet authority over science. At the beginning of every year, I see a physician and obtain an annual exam with blood work. Around 2022, I went for my physical exam, and the doctor said, "Well, you've never been administered an electrocardiogram (EKG), so let's do one of those just to make sure things look good." This is a test that traces cardiac electrical activity and is widely used to detect cardiovascular diseases such as arrhythmias, pericardial and myocardial diseases, and more (Rafie, Kashou, & Noseworthy 2021). I replied, "Sure." The doctor then proceeded to hook up electrodes to my chest to track the rhythm of my heart. After reading the results of the exam, she noticed an irregularity, as indicated on the chart. She stated that it was one of those things that "could mean something, or it could be nothing." Consequently, she sent me to a cardiologist, and that doctor again reviewed my results. This doctor confirmed the previous doctor's assessment but wanted to be on the safe side, so he scheduled me for an echocardiogram (echo) to, as he put it, get a closer look at my heart, measure it and the strength of it as well as the fluids around it. This was where things got interesting.

I laid back on my side as I watched my heartbeat on a computer screen. I could literally see a 3D image of my heart as the right and left ventricles opened and closed with each beat. The ventricles looked as if they had arms and hands opening every second to allow blood to flow to and from my lungs. Those hands reminded me of praising hands, like those of someone standing to their feet and shouting while worshiping the Lord. At that moment, I was overwhelmed with appreciation and admiration for God's craftsmanship. According to Levine (1997), the heart beats upwards of 3 billion times in a person's lifespan. This is astonishing, as all it takes is for one set of those praising hands to decide not to worship after one of those millions of times, let alone a billion...and its game over! There is no way I can be convinced that our hearts are set up like a perpetual lithium battery beating millions of times with two sets of hands praising for years with no breaks, and it's not influenced by divine authority. This is a good segway into our discussion of the "*Why*."

STAGE ONE

Why?

"He who has a Why to live can bear almost any how."

- Friedrich Nietzshe

I have been working in the field of mental health and substance use for roughly twenty-five years. As an agent of change, I have witnessed the progression of individuals who were in the pre-contemplation stage of change, with no intentions of making self-adjustments, to people thriving in the maintenance stage of change, having overcome the adversities of the change process to lasting transformation. In all cases and under any scenario, your *Why* is what not only gets you over the first hurdle to begin the transformation, but its magnitude is what will propel you through the trials and setbacks that are baked into the journey. Whether it be due to lack of adequate prioritization, lack of structure, complications with inattentiveness, or just a lack of self-discipline, your success with these functions always starts with your *Why*.

True Desire

This stage is about getting started. In my experience, of all the challenges, getting started with a change process is the most common and most difficult. People simply do not know where or how to begin. For some people, it boils down to them not having their true desires in alignment with the goals they set. For example, I have worked with clients who have asserted that they wanted to improve a relationship. As a result of that goal, they were given homework that they consistently did not complete. After some time, motivational interviewing disclosed that their genuine desire was not to maintain the relationship. In reality, they didn't like the sound of their true desire, so they said what sounded polite or acceptable to others. They attempted to convince themselves of a desire that was driven by external influences. Once they identified their honest objective, then the barriers to achieving the real mission could be addressed. Sometimes, guilt, embarrassment, shame, or lack of self-confidence are the driving forces dictating one's desire. In these instances, a person may not actually know what their desire is. In therapy sessions, I have heard, "I believe in my heart I should handle it this way, but I don't think that would be nice, and I would feel guilty about it." These types of revelations are good because they provide space to explore the pros and cons of making decisions so that a solid desire can be established.

Note: sometimes, it's critical to have a trained third party assist us along the way so that we don't waste our time convincing ourselves to do things that are not in our best interest and that we do not really yearn for ourselves. Thus, the first step of the "*Why*" stage is to search our gut and identify our genuine desire.

Your "Why" Must Be Greater

Once we have identified our true desire, we must identify why we want to achieve it. For this book and the MBCC, let's agree that our desire will always be something related to self-improvement. So, then the question becomes, why do we wish to improve ourselves? The most common response I receive to this question is "children." People will sprinkle in responses such as health, longevity of life, to improve specific relationships, or career advancement, but I never hear what matters most. When we think of our *Why*...why we would change our eating habits, or get up early in the morning... why we would begin to exercise or stop drinking alcohol…why we would quit cigarettes or marijuana… why we would check our attitude and monitor how we respond to people… why we would follow the steps of the MBCC… While it's acceptable for our *Why* to be attached to others such as children, spouse, or friends, loved ones cannot be the only or the primary reasons for our pursuit of self-growth. Additionally, while it's okay to desire to lose weight, fit into our clothes better, or get prepared for the summer, these cannot be the only or primary reasons for our self-development either.

On those cold winter mornings when we're warm and snuggled under the covers, and our alarm goes off, our *Why* must be greater than how we feel at that moment. At that moment, we may not care about how much we weigh or whether we look good in an outfit. As we have experienced, we can easily put off that goal for a later day or time. When the time comes to sacrifice that nap or extra sleep in the morning or adjust our evening routine by cutting short our favorite shows, we may not be thinking about the upcoming summertime, our kid's future, or how our spouse feels about our habits. More notably, if our *Why* is attached solely to other people, what happens if/when those people leave us? What happens when the kids go off to college and/or find their own place? What happens if our relationship doesn't work, or we relocate away from our friends? Or what happens if our loved ones simply do what many human beings do, which is to be inconsistent or fail us? We may not like the sound of this, but in truth, neither our mortal nor our eternal existence should hinge on having our family or friends. People and other external motivations are not imperishable. They come and go like the seasons and are momentary-like inspirations. While our *Why* can be influenced by external stimuli, it must always come back to an intrinsic motivation detached from anything or anyone else. The only everlasting stimulant is God, which brings me to my next point!

DR. ROBERT L. EVANS, III

The Divine in You

Every morning, my wife says to me, "I see the divine in you," and it's the divine in us that will be our most faithful *Why*. Just think for a second about how unfaithful and inconsistent our feelings are! They can change multiple times in the same discussion! If you struggle with believing whether you and everything you see is an accident or simply a result of a series of perfectly random occurrences, it will be difficult for you to digest what comes next. Spoiler alert! We should all share the same *Why*. There is only one unshakeable, unchanging, and consistently potent *Why*. This is the *Why* that moves me when I don't feel like it. The *Why* that overrides my mood, my comfort, and my desires. The *Why* that is too often overlooked and underrepresented. Ready?

I get up every morning not just because my wife lying next to me is watching or because my children in the next room are listening. Sure, these are precious factors, but ultimately, I move because I have the duty and honor of overseeing the twofold responsibility bestowed upon me by God himself. Firstly, I am responsible for protecting, nourishing, and building my temple, which is essentially his temple. We know this because Genesis 1:27 says God made us in his image. This means He is in each of us! Secondly, glorifying God in all that I do is woven into my purpose! I am on a mission to show others the power and glory of God through my actions, and this keeps me on point. In short, being his vessel is my *Why*. What other *Why* is more moving than that?

Note: If our intrinsic motivation to improve ourselves is not fueled by a desire to glorify God, we will never become self-fulfilled. We will always think and feel like we need more, and we will never experience a true appreciation of life and its purpose. We will experience an undying void in our hearts with no way to fill it, regardless of the amount of money we make or the volume of material possessions we amass.

"And God said, Let us make man in our image, after our likeness: and let them have dominion over the fish of the sea, and over the fowl of the air, and over the cattle, and over all the earth, and over every creeping thing that creepeth upon the earth. So, God created man in his own image, in the image of God created he him; male and female created he them"

(Genesis 1:27 KJV)

STAGE TWO

Intentionality

"Self-Awareness + Desire = Intentionality"

- Dr. Robert Evans III

To best prepare for the journey of transformation, there are some fundamentals to the process that we must first learn and embrace. Keep the discussion on perception and the mind in the backdrop. Before getting into the formula for the cheat code, it's imperative that I cover all the challenges to just getting started that I experienced and that I hear daily. I would hate for people to have a whole weapon and never get the chance to properly use it because they don't first understand the basics of weapon safety. You will shoot off your foot before I can show you the strategy to shoot from a mile away.

As we covered, the first challenge is people simply not having a solid *Why*. The next hurdle is to become intentional. While developing the skill of intentionality, we must understand how to align the desires of our hearts and minds with our actions. I call this process "mind & body alignment." We must understand and accept all three stages before getting into the fourth stage. Accordingly, let's get into intentionality and mind & body alignment so we can thoroughly enjoy the meat and potatoes in the fourth and final stage.

Self-Awareness

So, I went to trusty wordhippo.com, which defines intentionality as "The defining characteristic of the mental state of a person when deliberating about an intention." Then I said, "Well, let's look up intention." Wordhippo.com defines it as "The goal or purpose behind a specific action or set of actions." Then I said, "Well, let's complete the mission and look up intent." The two definitions that came up were: 1) "A purpose; something that is intended," and 2) "The state of someone's mind at the time of committing an offense." Of these definitions, the two concepts that stand out are *purpose* and *mind state*. To be intentional and not simply aimlessly behaving, one must move with purpose, on purpose.

To have a purpose is to have a direction... a target. As it happens, we can have a direction and we can have a target, but if we are unaware of our strengths and limitations, we will frequently miss our mark. Thus, to be genuinely intentional and purposeful starts with self-awareness. For example, if you want to become the best boxer, it will behoove you to be aware of your strengths and areas of development with respect to overall physical conditioning, hand/eye coordination, hand and foot speed, strength, intelligence, and rhythm. If you choose not to explore these areas before jumping in the ring with a trained fighter, you are asking for a world of hurt! The same goes for all areas of life, especially when it comes to the general navigation of adulthood.

In life, we are as successful as our awareness of what we need to improve and our willingness to do the necessary work.

If I had to sum up the reasons why people come to me for therapy in one word, it would be relationships. Usually, when the layers are peeled back, the anxiety (the number one complaint for my clients) that people feel, is related to relationships. Often, the depression that people feel and the anger they express are directly connected to relationships. When it comes to feeling overwhelmed or failing to effectively prioritize, it's usually due to a lack of boundary setting and relationship management. Broken relationships, parental relationships, spousal or romantic relationships, vocational relationships, fear of relationships, distrust of relationships, enmeshed and inappropriate relationships, loss of relationships, isolation from relationships, and all other relationships. Why are relationships relevant to self-awareness? The health, productivity, trust, direction, and overall success of a relationship are predicated on the self-awareness of the individuals in the relationship.

To be in a happy and thriving relationship, shouldn't we know what we are passionate about and what makes us tick? Wouldn't it make for great discussions with our partner if we know our triggers, if we are aware of any suppressed anger, or if we have past trauma hindering us from being emotionally available? If we have trouble trusting because of our previous experiences, won't that impact our ability to connect and build with our partner?

Tip: One of the first questions I tell people to ask when they are dating with the purpose of developing a long-term and healthy relationship is, "Tell me all of the things you need to fix or improve about yourself." Now, this may or may not be a first-date question. But it's definitely an "early in the getting to know you phase" question. This is a loaded question because the way it is answered reveals a tremendous amount of usable data to work with when deciding to move forward with this person. By the way, please know the answer to this question before asking it. Be the example of what you want from a potential partner. So, anyway, to answer this question effectively, the person must first have a level of emotional availability. A lack of emotional availability doesn't mean a person is broken. It just means that if you're looking for a long-term relationship, this person is not ready for it. Lack of emotional availability also speaks to a person's willingness to trust. If a person is not in a place where they are capable of trusting, they are not a good candidate for a relationship. Additionally, if they are hesitant to trust, they are more likely to not be someone you should fully trust because what I have seen is that these people keep their options open. This speaks to the critical urgency for us to be as self-aware as possible when attempting to build a lasting relationship.

Self-awareness of our strengths and areas of development impacts all aspects of our lives, and it is the first step to becoming intentional. Of course, to successfully complete a task, we need more than just the knowledge of what it takes to accomplish the goal. Likewise, for a relationship to work, it will require more than simply knowing our trauma and how it impacts our ability to trust, knowing what makes us anxious or afraid, or knowing what impedes our willingness or ability to properly express ourselves. This brings me to the next concept in the intentionality equation: Desire.

Desire

Let's pick up with the dating scenario, and let's say the person is special and can answer your loaded question. After you have asked, "So, tell me all of the things you need to fix or improve about yourself," your follow-up question is, "OK, so what have you been doing to fix those things?." Reminder: it is imperative that we have these questions already answered for ourselves. In fact, your ability to answer these questions will let you know your readiness for a long-term relationship. People quite often say they are ready, but in reality, they are not even close to being ready. They prematurely jump into a situation that they cannot be fully present for and wonder why their relationships don't last long. Pardon the digression! Now, you have asked your second loaded question, and just like the first, this one is a doozie!

When you ask the person, "What have you been doing?" it assumes the person has been actively doing something to fix their problems. The last thing we want is to hitch ourselves to a person who lives by the mantra, "This is how I have always been!" If the potential partner begins to answer this question with future intentions and not present action, that is an indication of their true desire. One thing about desire is it doesn't lie. What people often have a problem with is not following through with their desires. Rather, it's admitting that they are, in fact, following through with their desire to remain the same and not make the necessary changes. In many instances, people just don't like the fact that what they truly desire is not the most politically correct or socially acceptable thing. So, if the person is unable to speak to what they have been earnestly doing to manage or mitigate their known problems, they lack desire.

When our desire is absolute, there is no wavering.

To be fair, I should preference the relationship readiness discussion by saying an ability to effectively answer these questions is related to age and experience. I would expect a person in his/her forties that is intending to develop a lasting relationship, to already have these questions answered prior to getting into the relationship. However, a person in his/her early twenties gets some reprieve only because they likely have not experienced enough life to have the answers. Of course, it's contingent on experience and maturity, but in general, it would not be a red flag for someone in their twenties to still be figuring these things out. With that said, if you are reading this and you are in your twenties, you are probably an exception to the rule and need to connect with others who, like yourself, are interested in self-development. But let's just say you are the first to introduce to them the concept of self-development, your task is to evaluate their level of humility and willingness to grow. If they have it all figured out and are not open to enlightenment, you will be accepting a headache if you decide to pursue anything with them. That tip was for free!

Let's sum up the discussion on desire. We now understand that to be intentional about anything, we must first be aware of our history, our strengths, and our shortcomings. Then, we must decide what we want to do about it, despite the uphill battle it may take. Once we do an inventory of everything that has to do with our goal, we may realize, "Man, this will take a great deal of effort to accomplish." In the face of what it will take, we must still decide. What do we desire?

Quick story! As you can see by now, I love stories! I was putting together a presentation on managing implicit bias for professionals in law enforcement and other helping fields. In short, implicit bias is something that we all have. It is the unconscious view we have of people, places, and things that have been developed by the information and experiences we have had in relation to those things. For example, if all you see across multiple media outlets are young African American males carjacking elderly white women, you could quite reasonably begin to associate young African American males with being high-risk and violent offenders who should be feared, especially by elderly women. This is a natural process that is not attached to any particular race. The real offender is the media, but that's for another discussion. So, I developed steps to help professionals understand the process of developing implicit biases, but most notably, I developed a method to assist with combatting implicit biases. This is all relevant because the steps to mitigating implicit biases are similar to the intentionality equation. People must first be aware of their biases, and then they need to decide if they truly want to do something about it. What is their desire? Do they still want to treat people unfairly and undeservingly because of baseless stereotypes and disinformation, or do they want to begin to give people an opportunity to show who they are? If they make the decision to be intentional about change, it leads to other steps for a different discussion, but this is a good segway into the obstacles to being intentional.

Intentionality Haters
Feelings

Feelings are one of two things that get in the way of you being intentional. How many times have you been planning on doing something special for someone you care about, but the plans changed when that person did something to upset you? We are going to discuss emotions later in this book, but know this, the majority of people are led by their emotions. Meaning, approximately 90% of people allow their behavior and decisions to be dictated by their feelings (Kahneman & Tversky, 1979). This is a clear barrier to intentionality. Do not allow your feelings to stop you from following through with your plans to change.

The second we decide to become intentional; life will check the fabric of our desire and see just how serious we are.

In my 2021 book, *Run to the Pain*, I stated, "Whenever we make a definitive decision to change something in our lives, we will surely face adversity, and the test will be immediate and of equal measure." This is a universal law. So, always remember, **we will be tested as long as there is a test!** This means that as long as we struggle in areas of our lives that trigger negative emotions, we will be tested in those areas. When we do the work (seek help from a professional if needed), we will no longer view those areas as a test.

Tip: Before acting on a negative emotion, have a conversation before you show your hand. You may find out that your feelings are incongruent with the situation. For example, I have heard young people affectionally refer to each other as "fools." Needless to say, fool was not a term of endearment when I was coming up. However, knowing what you know now, if you were to be referred to as a fool by someone from Generation Z between the ages of 12 and 27, prior to allowing yourself to feel disrespected, try the "Pin in the Emotion" method.

Strategy: Put a Pin in the Emotion, Assess, Create (PAC)!

1) ***Pin the Emotion:*** When you figuratively get hit in the stomach by something someone says or does, and it generates a negative emotion, sit the emotion down before reacting. Unless the act is a blatant violation of your physical safety or a breaking of established trust, then move on to the next step.

2) ***Assess:*** Collect data! If something was said, find out if the person's intent was to hurt you. Let them know the message that was sent by their words and give them an opportunity to make corrections. Many times, people simply say things that are not in alignment with their true intentions.

3) ***Create:*** Develop a plan to move forward and ***Get out of your feelings!***

Distorted Thinking

The second thing that has the potential to impede our intentionality is counterproductive and often intrusive thinking. This is usually a result of an area of our life where we are unhealed. For example, one of my clients allowed her boyfriend to use her car to go to work. He worked a shift where he got off work in the middle of the night. One night, instead of coming straight home, he stopped at a gas station and convenience store. When he got home, my client confronted him with rage fueled by anxiety and past trauma. Due to unhealed wounds from a previous relationship, when her boyfriend failed to get home at the same time as in previous instances, she immediately thought that he was being disloyal and violating the trust of their relationship. Essentially, she punished him for the crimes of the previous relationship. It took a professional to help her realize the impact of her thinking and unhealed trauma on her current relationship.

Tip: Instead of acting on negative and deflating thoughts, sit the thoughts down and seek understanding. Like you had to do with the negative emotions, practice honest and transparent self-expression. Don't just run away with your thinking before having a discussion.

Strategy: Assess, Seek, and Keep It Moving (ASK)!

1) *Assess:* Do a quick assessment to see if your observation or thinking is related to a new or repeat offense. Is there evidence to

support your thinking? Is your thinking related to behavior that is egregious to the extent that it violates your dignity and is a deal breaker? If it is based on deal breaker behavior, does the person know from previous discussions your level of urgency regarding the behavior?

2) **Seek:** Have an adult conversation. Ask questions prior to disclosing your views about the situation. The answers you receive may resolve the situation and save you some embarrassment. Also, you want to get the person's raw response unencumbered by your opinion, otherwise you may never get that person's honest thoughts about the situation.

3) ***Keep it moving:*** The key is to process your thoughts and, if necessary, come to an agreement as to what changes need to be made and the steps to move forward. Once you have this, you need to move on and let the situation go. I will cover how to "let go" later. For now, remember that you cannot be ruled by thinking that

keeps you stuck. If people continue to violate your trust, hold them accountable, but if you are stopping your forward progress toward intentionality based on irrational and unfounded thinking, you are selling yourself short and sabotaging your progress.

"Despite the factors influencing who we have been, we must make a concerted effort to implement behaviors that will move us closer to that which we desire."

- Dr Robert Evans, III, *Run to the Pain*

STAGE THREE

Mind & Body Alignment (MBA)

"Nothing in life is as important as you think it is, while you are thinking about it"

- Daniel Kahneman, *Thinking, Fast and Slow*

As I previously mentioned, in 2020, the journey to become the best version of myself was kicked into overdrive. I went from running on the treadmill in a nice, comfortable gym to running outside on the concrete. Along the way, I went through various knee supports and running shoes. This is when I also became intimately familiar with my self-dialogue, that inner voice in my head that activates during interesting times. Prior to this, self-dialogue was one of those things that played in the background, like elevator music. I always knew it was there, but until then, I didn't realize the impact of the language, the tone, and the intent of my self-dialogue on my efforts to complete tasks and push myself beyond my comfort zone. For some reason, the volume of my inner voice turned up from level 1 or 2 to level 10.

At this point, without realizing it, I unlocked intentionality. Knowing what I was up against amidst the pandemic (Self-Awareness), I chose to pour into myself (Desire). I made a self-commitment to exercise daily and not permit any excuses, reasonable or otherwise, to stymie my progress. What I didn't realize was not only would I have to compete against the outside elements in combination with the pain of my physical reconditioning, but I would also have to contend with the persistently cynical voice in my head. This voice that was there to cheer me on and congratulate me when I was winning was the same voice that was discouraging me from reaching my goal. Well, the voice actually sounded encouraging. The caveat was it encouraged me to do the opposite of what I had already committed to doing. Instead of pushing me to endure the pain of growth, it was persuading me to rest more, take my foot off the gas, or take days off. I came to realize that the greatest battle I would have to face was the one with myself. I quickly learned that I needed to get both my mind and body on the same page. Sure, I was out there doing what I said I would do, but my mind was not yet fully accepting of this fact. Ultimately, "I needed to push myself physically to realign myself mentally" (Evans, 2021).

Storytime! One day, after a month or so of daily exercise, I began my usual 1.5-mile run, and as expected, I started talking myself out of the run. "Why are you doing this again?" the voice would say. Or "You know you can stop, and nobody would know, right?" I simply ignored the voice and kept up with my normal pace. Towards the end of the run, with about 100 meters left, I would typically sprint it out. This is where things got interesting. On this day, during the moment when I was supposed to pick up speed and kick with my last bit of energy, the volume of my inner voice rose to the maximum volume. "Slow down!" "Why are you doing this to yourself?" "Nobody is watching!" "You don't even have to finish!" Just a few of the "encouraging" statements that were playing like a drum in my mind. Oddly, while all this banter was swirling in my head, I could feel my arms begin to pump, and my legs begin to charge up! I picked up the pace on queue and finished just as strong, if not stronger, than ever before. It was at that moment that I realized, through consistency, I had conditioned my body to perform optimally, despite the noise of my inner voice. It wasn't too long after that before my inner voice started to change. The language was different. I learned how to turn down the volume of the voice that was rooting for my failure and turn up the voice that was telling me not to quit! I call that strategy "frequency management." What I now realize is that I had not only successfully evaded the influence of my negative voice, but I quelled the arrogance and pride in that version of me! I defeated him!

"Commit to the Lord whatever you do, and he will establish your plans" - Proverbs 16:3

For the mind & body alignment process to be successful, it will require two essential ingredients: self-commitment and consistency. The grit of consistency is fueled by our self-commitment, and with repetition, we will develop muscle memory that becomes autonomic: a habit. Ironically, we can develop a habitual routine physically before the thoughts driving our self-dialogue have even caught up. In other words, just as I experienced when my legs were increasing speed while my thoughts were still cynical, our aim is to develop a positive habit through consistency and, with time, allow our minds to catch up and become aligned. We simply need to be aware of, embrace, and trust the process.

Self-Commitment

We just identified the inner voice in your head is YOU. The caveat is depending on the messaging you receive, that voice is either that of the current version of you, or the new and improved future version. Both versions live in your mind. It's just that in the beginning of the MBA process, the current you is dominant until the new you takes the helm. You can tell the difference between the two voices because one will encourage you to remain in your current condition, avoid being uncomfortable, remind you of the unknown, and persuade you to be fearful. The other voice will be focused on doing something different so that you can achieve better results. This voice will insist that you push through pain and discomfort and refrain from quitting.

Whenever you embark upon a journey to improve any aspect of yourself, you are taking off your gloves and slapping the current you in the face, inciting a war! A war between the you who is comfortable and who doesn't want changes and the you who is ready for growth and willing to do what it takes to achieve it. So, take special care to listen and follow the voice of the best version of you. People don't have a problem with self-commitment. They are simply committed to the version of themselves they are most comfortable with. Remember, comfort is usually attached to being sedentary, so the comfortable and content version of you will stagnate your overall growth and the boundaries of your success.

Our bodies are designed to maintain homeostasis, and our brain and body want to remain at peace (Billman, 2020). They prefer to stay comfortable. At least, it appears that way due to the discomfort associated with any form of change. The truth is that discomfort and pain are, in many instances, correlated with growth and strength building. People just don't tend to view it that way. When we introduce anything new to our routine, we are essentially disrupting our mental and physical homeostasis or balance. When this happens, depending on our view of and willingness to embrace change, it triggers a chain of events. For those who don't do well with change, your mind deploys troops for mental warfare. The cozy and conservative troops who want to stay safe and keep things the same, or the progressive troops who are bold and want change. Still, for those of us who welcome change and see obstacles as opportunities for personal growth, when an unexpected disruption or a chance to do something new happens, mental troops are still deployed for war, but they are all on one accord and share the same goal to adjust to and learn from the new expectations as quickly as possible.

The first step to self-commitment is to identify which version of ourselves we are committing to. This may require some intense self-reflection, shadow work, and/or therapy to assist you with deconstructing your self-image and supporting you with embracing a new self identity. In my experience, people often remain stuck here, and they fail to get started with the change process because they have not yet fully let go of their well-constructed and well-loved image. An image they have been crafting for decades and one that they enjoy because of the love they receive from others.

Imagine if you are known as the life of the party amongst your friends and family. "Fun Bobby" is what everyone calls you, and you know that your energy level, attitude, and disposition are directly connected to you being under the influence of alcohol when you're at events. Over time, you begin to recognize challenges with relationships, work performance, stability, and failing to meet obligations. You then get arrested for driving while under the influence and are required to seek help. So, you seek therapy, and one of the goals developed is to quit alcohol. Here is where things get tricky. Some people think that in situations like this, the addict should be able to see all the damage done in their lives due to alcohol consumption, and they should be able to accept that alcohol is their enemy. While it is true that alcohol is a threat, it is merely an accessory to the addict's problems. In reality, the true enemy is the addict's self-identity. It's Fun Bobby, who the addict is committed to, and when it's time to end the relationship with alcohol, the addict believes that turning down the alcohol is a form of self-betrayal. To the addict, how could he turn his back on Fun Bobby after he has been there? They have been the entertainment for everyone, and they have had so many good times.

Give yourself permission to commit to the new you and release the old you just like an outdated version of a cellphone. This may not be easy, and again, it may require some assistance from a professional, but trust me when I say it can be done. I am proof of it, and I see the outcomes in my clients every day. Mind & body alignment requires intentionality. Be aware of the trials you will face, and how many of them will be self-inflicted. Don't allow negative self-dialogue to deter you from your goal. Understand that when you're beginning a change process, your body needs to be conditioned, and at times re-conditioned to adjust to the change. This means you will experience both mental and physical resistance, and that is to be expected. Don't read the challenges as signs to quit. Like in the case of exercise, muscle aches and soreness come with the soup! Your inner voice is going to tell you to put it off until later or remind you it's a holiday. Guess what, sometimes the reasons to postpone the start of your changes are reasonable. These are "Reasonable Excuses" by the way! It may be your birthday, or you may be on vacation. The gym may be closed due to the weather, or the library may not have electricity that day. Whatever you are attempting to change will, at some point, require you to go above and beyond to remain consistent, and now that you know it's part of the change process, you can exercise patience and stick to the script with grit and determination!

Self-commitment is the byproduct of having a solid and unwavering *Why*. A divine *Why!* When we're committed to God, and we understand and accept that God is in us, we will commit to ourselves, and we will prioritize ourselves first! Just as giving 10% of our earnings to God's work is a way to honor God and his word, so is following through with a commitment to ourselves and our word.

Tip: Self-commitment is the wellspring for self-trust. It starts with a commitment to our word, followed by consistency, which builds trust. **Self-Commitment + Consistency = Self-Trust.** Simply put, build self-trust by doing what you say you are going to do! Self-trust is crucial because it bleeds into so many other areas of our self-image, such as self-confidence, self-esteem, self-efficacy, self-value, and self-love.

"After God's word, nothing is more important than your word to yourself! If you can't trust your own word, it will be hard for you to trust others and for others to trust you!"

- Dr. Robert L. Evans, III

Consistency

Consistency is right at the top of the list of most common areas of needed self-development for my clients. It is the culmination of you doing what you say you are going to do and then rinsing and repeating it over and over again. It cannot be said enough that our *Why* is the foundation. For this section, the focus will be on ways to avoid and/or mitigate the unexpected and spontaneous challenges that hinder consistency. Let's dive into the significance of *structure* and *cockiness* and evaluate how these two things, if not properly managed, can encumber us from remaining true to our commitments.

Structure

When we are identifying our list of priorities and bringing order to our lives, remember there are two areas of our lives that need structure. There is the area of our lives that pertains to our *Organizational Health* (OH), and there is the area of our lives that pertains to our *Quality of Life* (QOL). It is important to distinguish these two areas because I see people typically entangle them and allow for one area to impact the other due to the overlap. The results of this intersection can be catastrophic.

The term organizational health can be used synonymously with holistic health. Think of yourself as the chief executive officer of an organization that is comprised of health departments. We all have a physical, mental, emotional, spiritual, and social health department, and all of them work together and are critically essential to our organizational health. We must implement a <u>daily routine</u> to intentionally address each of these health departments. Regardless of what we have going on in our lives, the vitality of these departments is what keeps us feeling balanced, sane, and fulfilled. We must have staple and immovable practices that we maintain without fail, regardless of a birthday, holiday, vacation, workload, or any other demands. When my clients come to me feeling overwhelmed with the demands of life, many times, it's because they stopped tending to their OH departments when life got hard. When the hurricane of life is coming at us with the wind speed of a category 5 storm, it's our daily routine and our commitment to the structure of our organizational health that keeps us grounded.

The QOL area of our lives consists of responsibilities such as work, school, children, or anything else that pulls our attention first thing in the morning and throughout the day and has us ruminating over it before bed or while attempting to get rest. These are demands that can drastically impact our lives if we do not manage them well, and they surely require our attention. They can also evoke a great deal of stress and anxiety because they are often tied to our finances and livelihood. However, we must keep QOL priorities separate from OH priorities because QOL demands can be unpredictable, inconsistent, and dynamic, while OH priorities must remain constant.

Check out how this works in real life. I have a client who is a college professor, and she is also pursuing her doctorate degree. She had been working her way through the mind & body alignment process and was becoming very consistent with exercise and a daily routine for her health departments. When classes for her students began after a semester break, the school failed to provide her with the credentials she needed so that she could get her students started with coursework. This was extremely frustrating for her, and she allowed the QOL and OH areas of her life to intersect, pulling her attention away from her already established routine for her OH departments. So, she stopped exercising and eating as planned (physical health), and she stopped her daily affirmations and anxiety management drills (mental & emotional health). As you can imagine, due to compromising her OH departments, an already frustrating situation became overwhelming and unbearable. In her words, she *"threw it all away!"*

Unplanned life events such as this one happen, and to maintain balance when they occur, we must remember our staple OH daily activities that are currently in place. Those things cannot be compromised. Once we compromise those activities, it causes a ripple effect that impacts the homeostasis of our lives. We must identify certain habits as *mandatory* and *nonnegotiable*. One way to accomplish this is to identify an activity that will address each health department and ensure that those activities are placed on the "essential activities" list. We cannot allow life events to punch us in the mouth and stop us from doing these identified activities. I have heard clients say, "Why follow through with a schedule if it's already thrown off?" Remember, just because a quality-of-life goal is thrown off and will get unexpectedly set back from time to time, it doesn't mean we get to toss out the organizational health priorities we can control. This belief, and others like it, will kill our consistency when life starts "lifing"!

Tip: Use a daily planner and block off time for the essential activities that address your OH departments. Block off times for your QOL priorities as well but place mental protection around the OH time blocks. Remain flexible when it comes to the QOL time blocks because things can happen that are not in your control. However, you have control over the flexibility of your OH time blocks, and the key is not to be flexible with those. Sometimes, people think if one thing on their calendar gets thrown off, their attitude will be impacted, and they will not show up as their best selves for the other activities. So, in turn, they scrap the whole calendar. There is some validity to this thought because I see people frequently allow their emotions related to one event to impact their performance in other areas of their lives. This is something we must be aware of a guard against, and above all, we must keep our daily organizational health practices.

Cockiness

In 1992, Prochaska, DiClemente, and Norcross wrote a paper on addictive behaviors and the trans-theoretical model (TTM) of change. In it, they explored five stages of the change process: the pre-contemplation, contemplation, preparation, action, and maintenance stages. I'm issuing a warning regarding the maintenance stage. According to Raihan and Cogburn (2023), this is the stage where people sharpen their ability to anticipate potential triggers and develop coping strategies to be proactive about refraining from behavior that will reverse the good progress they've made. Additionally, since it takes roughly 5 years of abstinence before the potential for a relapse diminishes to only 7%, it is incumbent upon people to develop an "action plan" that will support their success in sustaining the maintenance stage (Raihan & Cogburn, 2023).

Notice the word *action*, and remember, the same action required for us to make a change is vital to preserve that change. I have seen people do well to apply the tools needed to make a change, taste their desired results, and then completely fall off. When evaluating the reasons why these people returned to their recalcitrant behaviors, the feedback is commonly the same. They start to feel overly *comfortable, confident,* and *careless*, which ultimately leads to complacency. For example, people start missing doses of medication, become inconsistent with self-help groups, fall off from therapy, go back to old hangout spots, and essentially throw away the tools they used to successfully beat their undesirable habits. Hence, the second word to remember is *Cocky*.

Our immature, pitiful, and malignant behaviors represent the old version of who we are. Just because we have beaten him/her and been successful in making the changes we desire does not mean that version of us no longer exists. They may not currently have strength, but they are just like a cancer in remission, waiting for the moment to take back control of our lives. That version of us gains strength from our complacency resulting from our cockiness. I must give credit to one of my clients for the following quote. When we were processing his relapse, he came to realize that it was the old version of himself who reared his ugly face, and he stated, "*I can't let him trick me out of my spot!*" I loved that because that is exactly what will happen if we do not remain focused and tirelessly recommit to the improved version of ourselves. We will get tricked out of our spot! Lucky thing, the MBCC will provide a strategy for recommitting to the best version of ourselves daily, so we can reduce the likelihood of becoming cocky.

"Don't let the old you trick you out of your spot!"

Anonymous Client... you know who you are!

Tip: The inner voice you hear is YOU, and those are YOUR thoughts! The key is to learn how to manage your thoughts. First, understand that we all have intrusive and unwanted thoughts from time to time. Sometimes, we have thoughts that are entirely contrary to our beliefs, morals, and principles. Just remember, you do not have to attach yourself to your random thoughts. This is a good segway into the self-commitment section, but first, here is a quick therapeutic tool!

Strategy: Thought Management!

1) ***Thought Stopping:*** When you have a negative or self-sabotaging thought pop into your head, tell yourself to "Stop thinking like that!" Some people have become so accustomed to talking down to themselves that they don't even realize they do it. So cynical that any opportunity to offer themselves encouragement, they take that moment to tell themselves what

they cannot do or how incompetent they are. Some thoughts happen so common that you can tell yourself to stop thinking that way, and it won't be difficult to move on. Your next step will be to condition your inner voice to talk nicely to you.

2) **Thought Replacement:** For other thoughts, it's more effective to have a replacement thought. For example, replace a sentence like, "Man, you won't be able to finish this race!" with one like, "Wait, but you finished a bunch of races before this one, so you can finish this one too!"

3) **Thought Passing:** I like to refer to some intrusive thoughts as "bully" thoughts! These are the ones that you know are coming, and you haven't been able to avoid them. These thoughts often generate anger or frustration in you because you don't want to think that way. For these, if you get upset with yourself for having the thought, if you start asking yourself, "Why am I thinking this way?" or if you attempt to investigate the thought in any way, you

will give breath and life to the thinking, and it will grow roots in your mind. Once the thought has roots, it will be hard to shake it. For this reason, when these thoughts happen, you can simply let them pass. Don't give the thought any energy, and don't quiz yourself about thinking that way. An example of this is when I travel over large bridges, I frequently think about driving off the bridge or experiencing a collision with someone who is not paying attention on the other side of the road. However, I learned to let the thought come and go without giving it any mental space to pitch a tent and camp out. I let it pass and simply shift my thinking to something productive.

"Remember, your brain and body will adjust to the condition you keep it in."

- Dr Robert Evans, III

STAGE FOUR

Inqubo

("Process" in the Zulu Language)

"Just as every person's fingerprint is unique and specific to their identity based on a precise skin pattern, the MBCC is also very specific and requires a combination of activities for it to be viable. - Dr Robert Evans, III

So, let's do a quick recap so that we will be assured of the fundamentals of what we are about to cover. The overall mission of this book is to teach how to successfully initiate and maintain a transformational change process. A specific strategy for this will be covered, and this strategy provides us the capability to improve anything about ourselves. You name it, and it covers it, but there are foundational prerequisites that must be clearly understood first; otherwise, simply providing you with a life-changing tool would set you up for failure. It would be like giving you the keys to a Ferrari when you have never driven a car before. If you don't even know how to properly accelerate or brake, what benefit to you would it be to have the keys to basically drive a missile?

With that said, we started this off with a discussion about our *Why*. This is because I desire for us to experience lasting change and not something that is sparked by the new year or a season. Our

Why is not only where it starts, but it is going to push us when we don't feel like it. It's going to be the thing that gets us out of bed and the thing that keeps us faithful to our word. Our *Why* is the cement foundation for our consistency. After discussing the *Why* we should get up in the morning, we then learned how to *intentionally* complete a goal. We reviewed the elements of intentionality as well as the "haters" that stand in the way of us being intentional. We then went over the process of mind & body alignment so that we can be prepared for the mental challenges that come with our attempt to answer our *Why* with intentionality. This was crucial so that we could understand the change process and not quit halfway through our transformation. After that, we processed self-commitment followed by consistency, and along the way, we discussed some tools to apply immediately to our lives.

Now it's time to explore how the brain and body function so that we will see how the elements of the MBCC work together to become a tool with the power to essentially transform who we are. Our body is the most wonderfully made work of art in existence. All things within our bodies have a purpose and work in concert for our good! As I previously touched on in the introduction, our mind is the motherboard that houses our perception, and our perception of any given moment is what determines our behavior/how we choose to respond to that moment. Another huge aspect of this psycho-social activity is *Emotion*. We are talking about a transformation of our entire being. How we think, what we believe, how we view ourselves, and how we behave and respond to unpleasant or undesirable events and people. To do this, it is a must that we talk about a couple of key essentials that will tie all the MBCC elements together. Because most people allow their emotions to dictate their behavior, we must touch on emotional regulation. This will be followed by an overview of the vagus nerve and vagal tone, which will show us how both our mind and body are impacted by the MBCC. Finally, we will review the different elements of the MBCC and learn how to combine them all in a single inqubo.

Emotions

Our neuroception or lens that we see the world through is developed from our experience, knowledge, and implicit clusters of core beliefs that we have come to embrace both consciously and subconsciously (Porges & Stephen, 2004). First, we encounter an event or moment that enters our awareness through our senses and is translated and processed in our mind/thalamus and sent to the appropriate department of the brain for further evaluation. Depending on what we have come to <u>believe</u> about the current moment, it will be sent to the prefrontal cortex for stimulating and thought-provoking internal/self-dialogue or sent to the amygdala to generate an emotional response that corresponds with the event (Šimi´c et al., 2021). This process has been well-studied for decades.

MIND AND BODY TRANSFORMATION

In 1884, William James stated, "bodily changes follow directly the perception of the exciting fact, and that our feeling of the same changes as they occur is the emotion." In other words, we tell ourselves how to feel.

When my oldest son was a baby, I already had this understanding of pain and emotions and how we determine our responses based on our interpretation of every moment. So, when he fell, I never ran over like it was a scary moment. I always made the moment fun and told him to "hop up!" Thus, he learned to interpret falling as something that wasn't scary, but an acceptable aspect of life. He also learned to process pain in a unique way and developed a mental toughness very early. Just remember, we must give ourselves permission to feel the way we do, and furthermore, we get to assign how much power that feeling possesses over our behavior.

DR. ROBERT L. EVANS, III

Targeting Emotions

Leonard Berkowitz and colleagues believed that people could be preconditioned to express a positive or negative emotion towards others and tested this hypothesis via an experiment that incorporated the manipulation of physical sensations. Female university students were placed under either a physically painful condition with their hands being submerged in a tank of extremely cold water or a soothing condition with their hands in a tank of warm water. They were then tasked with issuing punishments or rewards to other female participants in the experiment. As you can imagine, the group of women who had their hands submerged in painfully cold water were more likely to punish the other participants, while those who had their hands in warm water were more likely to issue rewards to the other participants. Apparently, the painful condition activated "aggression-related expressive-motor reactions," which are aggressive responses that happen subconsciously (Berkowitz, Cochran, & Embree, 1981). What does this all mean? Essentially, we can subconsciously condition ourselves to respond to people in either a positive or a negative way without even realizing it. Well, if we can do this involuntarily, what would happen if we were intentional about targeting our future responses to people or events?

How many times have you come home from work after a frustrating day and took your frustrations out on your family by either not speaking to them, shutting them down, being rude to them or just being a jerk? Or how about vice versa and taking your home life to work where your colleagues or clients pay for your frustrations? For some people, they intentionally choose to take out their frustrations on the people they love and care about. This happens for various reasons. Clients have stated that they thought their loved ones should be the ones to accept them and their frustration while they pretend to be someone different for the rest of the world. This is an example of "emotional displacement," where people take out their anger and negative emotions on innocent people instead of the individual(s) who are truly connected to the frustration (Lin, Cheng, Sun, Feng & Bai, 2024). Usually, this happens if a person wants to avoid conflict with someone in a position of authority, so they aim their rage towards others who don't pose a threat. The MBCC will show you how to manage these situations so that you will target or release your frustrations in an optimal manner and not toward innocent bystanders. By the end of this book, we will have learned the magic of intentionality and preparing your thoughts and emotions for those situations and people who you already know you have a problem with.

Be the movie director of your day or be an extra in someone else's movie!

Core Beliefs

The MBCC is a method that helps us shape and refine our core beliefs, which are "fundamental, absolute, and lasting comprehensions that a person develops about him or herself, others, and the world" (Osmo et al., 2018). They are essentially the building blocks of our perception, which drives our thinking and begets our emotions, thus influencing our behavior. This quick illustration proves to you that if we can control our core beliefs, we can control our behavior. Imagine yourself holding an infant in your hands that is just beginning to gain some leg strength. This is one of the cutest babies you have ever seen. The baby is bouncing up and down on your lap as you hold their hands. The baby is smiling and laughing, and you are enjoying the moment. You go in to kiss the baby's neck to get a reaction out of the baby, and the baby bursts out laughing and starts slapping your face. At that moment, how do you respond?

a) Slap the baby in retaliation.

b) Toss the baby in the air and punt the baby like a professional football player.

c) Yell at the baby in anger.

d) None of the above because it's just a baby.

Ok, now imagine you are sitting at lunch with a friend or colleague, and that person turns and slaps you in the face with extreme force. Something like how Will Smith slapped Chris Rock. At that moment, how do you respond?

a) Slap your friend back in retaliation.

b) Pick up something to break over your friend's head.

c) Do your best to end your friend's life with your bare hands.

d) All of the above because your friend obviously lost their mind.

What thoughts were going through your minds in either scenario? If you reacted differently to the alternative circumstances, what thoughts made you come to different conclusions? This was the same physical attack, but you more than likely came up with a different response depending on the situation. When I posed this scenario to an audience before, I did hear a woman surprisingly say she would slap the child back. The reality is that no matter what your answer was in response to either event, it was your core belief about that situation that dictated your response. If you believe that children should never hit their parents or adults no matter how old they are, then you are more inclined to discipline the baby. Or if you believe that your friend is suffering from an impaired mental state, then you might decide not to retaliate after getting hit. Again, it is your core belief that informed your response to this and will continue to influence your future responses. The MBCC will provide a mechanism to help you change any core beliefs that are counterproductive and in the way of your growth and success.

Vagus Nerve

The cheat code is dubbed *Mind & Body* because not only does it help you to "make up your mind," but it also assists you with becoming physically fit. Additionally, as we will soon see, the brain and body have a bi-directional relationship, so with the MBCC, when you improve your mind, you improve your body, and vice versa.

The brain and spinal cord are connected to the rest of the body by over 7 trillion nerves, sending communication by way of electrical impulses. This, our *nervous system*, is how we interface with the world around us, and it is comprised of two parts: the central and peripheral nervous systems. The *central nervous system* (CNS) consists of the brain and spinal cord, while the peripheral nervous system (PNS) "comprises 12 pairs of cranial nerves, 31 pairs of spinal nerves, the ganglia associated with the cranial and spinal nerves, the right and left sympathetic chains and their ganglia, and the pelvic parasympathetic nerves" (Bazira, 2021). Both the CNS and PNS work cooperatively to successfully govern the functioning of the human body.

The cranial nerves are a set of 12 paired nerves resting in the back of our brain. Amongst many other things, cranial nerves help us process our senses, which is a mountainous task in and of itself. They also send messages from the brain to the face, neck, and torso, so we display expressions to represent our interpretation of our internal and external experiences. The *vagus nerve* (VN) is the 10th cranial nerve, and it is the longest and most elaborate of all cranial nerves. It extends from its origin in the brainstem through the neck and the thorax down to the abdomen. Also known as the "wanderer nerve" due to its length, the VN relays a vast range of signals from the brain to the digestive system and organs and vice versa. Accordingly, it is the primary mode of transportation on the "brain-gut axis," which is the bi-directional communication highway between the brain and the gastrointestinal tract (Breit, Kupferberg, Rogler & Hasler, 2018; Bazira, 2021). As the primary facet of the PNS, the VN assists with the oversight of bodily functions such as mood, digestion, heart rate, respiratory rate, immune response, and reflex actions like coughing, sneezing, swallowing, and vomiting. Remarkably, the essential role of the VN is to "bring information from the inner organs such as the gut, liver, heart, and lungs to the brain" (Bazira, 2021). Bear in mind, the amygdala, which is known for its role in the generation of emotions, is what modulates the activity of the vagus nerve (Breit et al., 2018; Bazira, 2021).

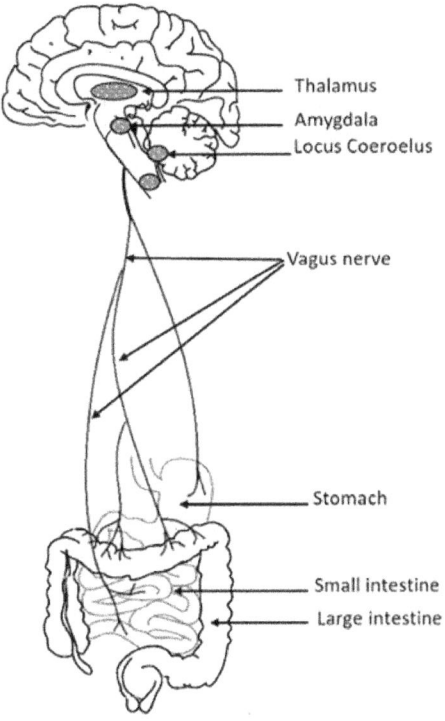

How is the vagus nerve connected to the MBCC, and what function does it have to facilitate mind and body transformation? Well, I'm glad you asked. As previously mentioned, the brain-gut axis permits a bidirectional relationship between the brain and the gastrointestinal tract. The brain-gut axis monitors "physiological homeostasis" and essentially relays messages back and forth from the brain to the gut to tell the body whether it's time to fight, run, or perform. Depending on the messages sent along the axis, the immune system may activate, and the enteric reflex system will either trigger a gastrocolic response and give you the urge to hit the toilet or an enterogastric reflex and shut down the stomach cramps because it's game time or signal the enteroendocrine system to release necessary hormones for strength and endurance (Breit et al., 2018; Sharkey, Keith, Mawe & Gary, 2023).

The brain-gut axis includes the brain, spinal cord, the autonomic nervous system, and the <u>hypothalamic-pituitary-adrenal (HPA) axis</u>. The vagus nerve is involved with the activation and regulation of the HPA axis, which is the quarterback of the body's stress response system (Bazira, 2021). **The HPA axis just happens to be the secret ingredient of the MBCC.** This will all begin to make sense as we tie in the other aspects of the cheat code.

Vagal Tone

We can't discuss the vagus nerve and not touch on the *vagal tone*. Researchers have measured vagal tone by "resting heart rate, heart rate recovery, heart rate variability, and baroreflex sensitivity" (Thayer & Lane, 2007). It is a measure of our cardiovascular health. Essentially, the health of our overall heart functioning reflects our command of vagal tone. What's important about this is that vagal tone has been referred to as the "biological correlate of emotion regulation" (Messerli-Bürgy, N., et al., 2020). In other words, the strength of our heart is directly correlated to our ability to regulate our emotions. Messerli-Bürgy et al. found that low vagal tone, or decreased cardiovascular health, is associated with poor emotional regulation in children and serves as a stress sensitivity marker. High vagal tone, or improved cardiovascular health, suggests a "high capacity for stress, change and challenges, and a higher capacity for rest, recharge and recovery." Of course, they found that low vagal tone means the opposite, in that children were less stress tolerant, struggled with embracing change, and found it difficult to rest, recharge, and recover. Decreased vagal functioning is also associated with an increased risk of heart disease and increased risk for morbidity and mortality (Thayer & Lane, 2007). Other benefits of high cardiac vagal tone are improved executive functions such as increased cognitive flexibility, or an ability to adapt thoughts and behaviors to changes in the environment, increased inhibitory control, or an ability to willfully control impulses, thoughts, and emotions, and increased affective empathy, or being able to connect to the emotions of others (Scrimin, Patron, Peruzza, & Moscardino, 2020).

This information about vagal tone is relevant to our discussion because research suggests that vagal tone is directly correlated with all things transformational. Heart disease, hypertension, diabetes, high cholesterol, and mortality rates are all impacted by high or low vagal tone (Thayer & Lane, 2007). We also know that vagal tone is measured by overall heart health. So, knowing the benefits of high vagal tone and the role of the vagus nerve in our brain and gut relationship, the logical question then becomes, "How do we strengthen the vagus nerve and vagal tone?"

To answer this question, we are going to jump into the five essential elements of the Mind & Body Cheat Code. As a reminder, to get the results of the MBCC, we can always do any of the five elements individually or with any number of combinations, and while we will still receive positive results towards making changes in our lives, we will not achieve the results that only the MBCC can produce. For those of us who have watched the Marvel Avengers movies, we know that the infinity stones were so rare and powerful as individual stones that they were scattered across galaxies so that they could not be collected and combined. Possession of the time, space, mind, reality, power, and soul stones individually was trouble, but when they were combined in the infinity gauntlet, the individual in its possession was the most power in the universe.

This is how I feel about the elements of the MBCC. Each one is an infinity stone, and the person who collects them and combines them must be ready for the power they possess. This is why it was important for us to go through how to get started with the change process, and why it was relevant to review the potential pitfalls and barriers to lasting change and consistency. Now, it's time to put those concepts into full effect so that we can use the combined power of each element of the MBCC to achieve our goal of long-term self-transformation.

"Physical fitness is mainly, although not entirely, determined by physical activity patterns that people perform over recent weeks or months."

- Scrimi, 2020

Infinity Stone #1

I know my clients get tired of hearing this, but hey, it's evidence-based and backed by research when I say exercise is essential to a long, healthy, and emotionally regulated life (Scrimin et al., 2020). I really didn't want to discuss exercise first because that's the one thing people don't want to hear when it comes to a transformation process. It's one of the greatest challenges for people to conquer. So, in true *Run to the Pain* fashion, it's only right that physical fitness is the first of the five infinity stones. Honestly, physical fitness is the answer to the question in the previous section asking,

"What strengthens vagal tone?," so I kinda had to make it the first stone. It just so happens that it fits to hit you with the most challenging stone first.

For those of you who struggle with regular exercise, you're going to be tempted to throw down the book now and walk away just because you see that physical fitness is a requirement. You are not alone because while people usually don't have a problem incorporating the other infinity stones, when we get to the exercise portion of the strategy, they begin to shrink. If that's you, here is where your *Why* kicks in, and where you must become intentional! Get out of your feelings and don't allow distorted thinking to deter you! Remember the mind & body alignment process! Can you imagine if this book started off with the infinity stones without preparing you for what you're getting yourself into? Luckily, we are having a well-balanced meal! Now if you skipped your veggies and jumped right into the main course, the crux of the code, then you may want to go back and have your appetizers and side dishes!

Remember, when it comes to our physical health department, we experience a cumulative effect. This means our overall physical health improves as we continue to chip away at it. We simply need to start at any point and slowly work from there. This means throwing away the lofty goals of lifting so much weight or losing so many pounds and reducing the goal down to plainly being consistent. Consistently showing up for yourself will generate a steady stream of positive results. When I started my daily pushup routine in 2023, my daily count was fifty pushups. That increased to 100 pushups, and from there, each week, I added 10 pushups. Now, I'm at 300 pushups daily. This is a result of consistently showing up for myself and nothing more. My only goals have been consistency and remaining committed to my word. Once we get into the requirement to access the HPA Axis during exercise, we will learn ways to do this, even for those of us who are completely out of shape, so don't throw in the towel!

The heart is the most integral muscle in our bodies, and like any other muscle, the only way to strengthen it is to exercise it. There is no way around it. Researchers have found that physical fitness moderates the association between cardiac vagal tone and inhibitory control. Inhibitory control is "defined as the ability to deliberately control or inhibit dominant or automatic behaviors, responses or thoughts" (Messerli-Bürgy et al., 2020; Scrimin et al., 2020). In 2020, Scrimin et al., measured physical fitness in participants by running them through a number of physical activities, and what they found is that those with increased fitness results also had higher levels of:

- self-esteem
- academic performance
- executive functioning (EFs)

- cognitive functioning
- mental flexibility

Increased fitness also resulted in decreased symptoms of depression.

Note: Running has been shown to have stunning results with respect to providing an opportunity for emotional regulation. We will revisit this discussion when we talk about the body's acute stress response, and then the relevance of exercise in the MBCC will all make sense.

Tips:

1. Don't wait until you feel motivated or when there is a "good" time to start. There is never a better time to start than right now.

2. Don't rely on other people for motivation. It's cool to set up an accountability partner or group to get you going, but consistency will come with a self-commitment first. Not a group commitment.

Without a self-commitment, eventually, you will say, "fu&% that group!"

3. Don't set unreachable short-term goals.

4. Just Start!

"It was Wilhelm Reich who discovered that deep breathing exercises give access to deeply pent-up feelings which the patient has blocked by anxiously constricting his aerial interchange with the world."

- Dublin, 1976

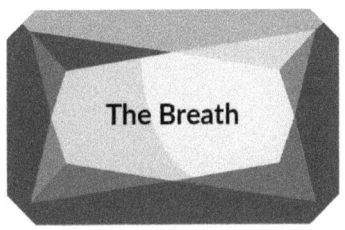

Infinity Stone #2

Life begins and ends with the breath. When a baby is born, the clapping and smiles don't start until the baby takes his/her first breath, and the time of death is not called until we take our last breath and our heart stops. What we often fail to acknowledge is that all breaths between the first and the last are just as significant. If only everyone knew just how powerful each breath was. When we take a breath (inspire), we breathe in oxygen, our heart rate increases as our diaphragm expands, and the oxygen is processed through our lungs. We then breathe out carbon dioxide (expire) as our heart rate decreases. This entire physiological process is called respiratory sinus arrhythmia (RSA) (Rassler, Blinowska, Kaminski, & Pfurtscheller, 2023).

RSA is the body's natural process to breathe in what we need to survive and breathe out what will kill us if we do not release it. If we don't breathe in enough oxygen, we won't make it long, and if we don't expel enough carbon dioxide, we will perish from the toxicity. RSA has been historically used as a measurement tool for vagal tone and cardiovascular strength (Rassler et al., 2023). This shows a connection between diaphragmatic breathing and vagal tone, which we have learned is directly connected to emotional regulation. Speaking of emotional regulation, researchers have found that emotions such as fear and anxiety can lead to shortness of breath (Levenson, Ekman, & Ricard, 2012). Additionally, individuals with high anxiety experience an inverse RSA effect where their heart rate decreases during inspiration and increases during expiration (Rassler et al., 2023). This is significant because it explains why people having anxiety attacks have trouble relaxing themselves. Their hearts are literally beating faster instead of slower with each breath, which keeps them in a heightened state of arousal.

Research suggests that people can better manage stress and anxiety by taking a few minutes to practice diaphragmatic breathing regularly. Taking control of breathing during heightened arousal states can redirect the flow of emotions (Levenson et al., 2012). Meditation, which involves controlled breathing, has been studied for decades and has been credited with many health benefits (Al-Hussaini et al., 2001; Levenson et al., 2012; Siehl et al., 2023). Vipassana means to "see things as they really are" (Al-Hussaini et al., 2001). This is a form of meditation that aims to improve concentration and self-awareness through mindfulness of the interaction between one's physical sensations and one's mind (Al-Hussaini et al., 2001). Levenson et al., looked at two kinds of meditation (open presence and focused) to check the influence they may have on the body's "acute stress response." Open presence meditation is defined as "open focused and fluid attention," while focused meditation requires continuous focus on a single object or event. They found that experienced meditators manage their subjective emotional experience and their physiological activity while under emotional distress better than those who don't meditate. Also, neuroimaging revealed that experienced practitioners of vipassana meditation had greater gray matter concentrations in the regions of the brain that are thought to be activated during meditative states (Levenson et al., 2012) Larger gray matter concentrations have been associated with improved emotional regulation (Siehl, Zohair, Guldner & Nees, 2023). Researchers also studied the impact of open presence and focused meditations on five symptoms of the body's acute stress response to include cardiac health. They subsequently found that both forms of meditation significantly reduced symptoms of the acute stress response. We will discuss the acute stress response later, as it is an essential ingredient in the MBCC.

The breath infinity stone is critical to the MBCC because a command of the breath is essentially a command of vagal tone. What is unique about the cheat code is that rather than practicing controlled breathing while resting or in a calm state (meditation), it requires an increased heart rate to provide the simulative effect necessary for optimal emotional training. Later, we will discuss how to take advantage of the RSA process to breathe in and out much more than oxygen and carbon dioxide. Remember, there are various combinations of individual stones that can help with emotional regulation and a transformative process. However, there is no other combination outside of the MBCC that will provide the same psychological and physiological effects simultaneously. You must collect all the infinity stones!

Tips:

- This is an easy one to practice. Start with when you open your eyes in the morning and before you close them at night. Breathe into your diaphragm to maximize the amount of oxygen that enters your body. If you have never intentionally done this before, place one hand over your belly and the other over your chest. Take a deep breath. You will notice that the hand on your chest did all the moving. Now practice taking a deep breath and only making your belly expand while keeping the hand on your chest still. When you get good at it, the hand on your chest won't move at all.

- When we get into the practice of the MBCC, we will be intentionally increasing our heart rate so that we can bring it back down with controlled breathing. I discovered through countless attempts at controlling my breathing while at a heart rate of 160-180 beats per minute (BPM) that taking huge breaths both in and out while my HR was that high did not bring down my HR quickly. Conversely, it stayed elevated. Once I understood the RSA process, I realized that if I took big breaths in, it would keep my HR raised, so I learned to take short breaths during inspiration, and instead of blowing out big during expiration, I simply let the air release. Again, this process became easier over time, but in the beginning, due to having decreased physical conditioning, cardiovascular strength, and vagal tone, I was focused more on catching my breath than on thinking. And guess what? While your heart is about to jump out of your chest, it is the perfect time to practice thinking! We will get into this more later when we discuss the simulation process.

"Self-affirmed people are freed from the need to self-protect, and they can process otherwise threatening information in a receptive and less biased manner."

- Strachan et al., 2020

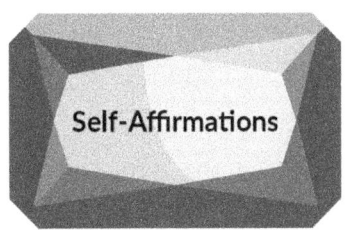

Infinity Stone #3

One morning, after my wife Von and I greeted each other as usual with "Good morning, Queen!" and "Good morning, King!" Von asked me, "So, how do you feel?." She asked me this because just a couple of days before that, I received some troubling news when I went for my annual physical exam. I felt some tightness in my stomach, and I didn't know whether it was a muscle strain from exercise or if there was a greater concern. I had the doctor feel my stomach, and her exam was inconclusive, so she sent me for further testing. My main concern was possibly having to break my streak of pushups and sit-ups, which had been going strong for many months. So, when Von asked me how I felt, my initial response was "disappointed." Now, prior to her asking me that question, I was moving around normally that morning at my usual pace and cadence. However, the moment I affirmed myself as "disappointed," I began to feel my head tilt forward, my shoulders started to hunch, and my demeanor shifted from sturdy to fragile. It's a good thing that I regularly practice mindfulness because I instantly recognize what is happening as it is taking place. My body was attempting to match the word I proclaimed over my life. I then thought to myself that word wasted no time before it began to poison me both emotionally and physically. I subsequently changed my identity from disappointed to hopeful. That was good because it stopped the initial depression of my emotional state and disposition. However, the effects of my original affirmation did not reverse until I proclaimed myself to be powerful. Side note: After obtaining an ultrasound and a computed tomography (CT) scan, I received a clean bill of health. I thank God too, because against my wife's advice, I never stopped my pushups and sit-ups. I just couldn't jeopardize my streak because of an inconclusive exam. I never lost faith and leaned into my *Why*!

A "self-affirmation is an act that affirms one's self-worth, typically by having individuals reflect on personally important values and strengths, which can give one a broader view of the self" (Łakuta, 2020). The above situation was so profound because I was able to experience the potency of both positive and negative self-affirmations. Almost everything we say is an affirmation, and affirmations can be both uplifting and deflating. Positive and negative words have the same potential for influence. Self-identifying words impact our mind, body, and spirit, and the second we affirm a label over our presence, our body immediately begins to adjust to the label. This is one of the reasons I don't usually inform my clients of a clinical diagnosis. I found that people displayed a tendency to own the diagnosis and use it as a justification for maladaptive behavior. I focus on changing behaviors and not curing a diagnosis.

Let's look at this from a different angle. If you say you feel abandoned, I suspect that not only will your demeanor begin to match that statement, but you may start to behave in a way that aligns with that self-affirmation. You may find yourself isolating, having trust issues, and sabotaging your friendships. Think about how quickly my demeanor began to shift after I identified myself as disappointed. Now think about how many people go for days, weeks, months, and years telling themselves something self-destructive, demeaning, limiting, and/or discouraging. For those people, the poison has likely become a part of their very existence. Their identity may even depend on it. Now it's time to turn the table! Check the below benefits of positive self-affirmations.

Positive Self-Affirmations [1]

- Reduce the effect of negative emotions
- Broaden a person's overall perspective
- Moderate sensitivity to self-threatening words
- Improved self-worth
- Improved stress management
- Improved academic performance
- Improved self-control
- Improved self-esteem and positive mood
- Improved relational security for insecure people
- Improved social interactions
- Improved self-image

---

[1] (Cohen & Sherman, 2014)

Negative Self-Threats[2]

- Negatively biased and self-focused attention
- Negative social interpretation biases
- Negative evaluative feedback
- Self-rejection
- Increased self-reported anxiety
- Increased social anxiety
- Decreased emotional regulation
- Decreased self-esteem

Tips:

- Practice positive self-affirmations 3x daily for 2 weeks to see results in the area of your life you are affirming

- Remember, we are designed in God's image, so we are intended to be an extension of him. When we are not affirming power and

---

[2] (Schulz, Alpers, & Hofmann, 2008; Cohen & Sherman, 2014)

advancement over our lives, we are not affirming God. When we succumb to negative self-threatening dialogue, we are not only hindering our best selves from shining through, but we are talking negatively to and threatening God. Consequently, at that point, we have become a weapon for the adversary. If we are not respectfully speaking to the divine in ourselves, we are uplifting the adversary within us. So, ask yourself, "Whose weapon are you?"

"Visualization meditation is a technique where the individual utilizes their imagination to create the things they want in their life."

- Prabu & Subhash, 2015

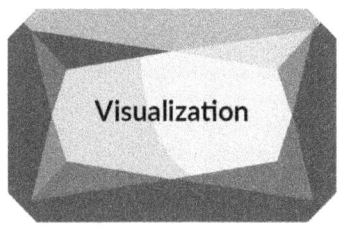

Infinity Stone #4

We had a great discussion on perception to start this book, and we learned that our perception is our reality. A major influence over our perception is what we visually see. What we see with our eyes closed can be just as influential as what we see with our eyes open. In fact, sometimes, while our eyes are wide open, we are watching a video playing in our minds, and we have completely tuned out of what is truly in front of our faces (Sun, He, Chen, Yang, Wei & Qiu, 2022).

The profound influence of visualization on our overall health and behavioral outcomes has been studied extensively across various professions (Botvinick & Cohen, 1998; Yao et al., 2019; Fadare et al., 2022; Niveau et al., 2022; Aksu & Ayar 2023; Kuriyama et al., 2023) Within the field of psychology, sometimes referred to as "guided imagery," visualization has been used as a therapeutic tool during meditation and has been shown to improve self-esteem and decrease depression, anxiety and stress (Niveau et al., 2022; Aksu & Ayar, 2023). "Visualization meditation directly affects the autonomic nervous system as it creates a *perception* in the body that there is an actual external stimulus and induces a response (Prabu and Subhash, 2015)" (Aksu & Ayar, 2023). Visualization has been studied and used by sports psychologists to assist athletes across almost all sports in improving their performances (Fadare et al., 2022). In the medical field, nurses and medical students have used visualization during training to improve the medical professionals' performance when conducting procedures (Prabu & Subhash, 2015; Kuriyama et al., 2023). Researchers have also studied the influence of video games and found a statistically significant correlation between violent video games and aggression.

What we see is so influential over our reality that we can witness something happening to someone else and feel a physiological response as if the event happened to us. Gong et al., (2022) discussed the concept of "interoception," which is the sensation of the physiological state inside one's body. They found that what we visualize can generate a physiological response and, ultimately, regulate the sensation of pain. In 1998, Botvinick and Cohen conducted a prominent study referred to as the "rubber hand illusion" and found that participants experienced a physical sensation based on what they were watching take place to something that appeared to be their hand. In reality, what they were viewing was a rubber hand that did not belong to them. This was a remarkable experiment incorporating visualization and interoception.

This is all relevant to the mind & body cheat code because visualization is a requisite activity within the strategy. Like the stones that preceded it, physical fitness, the breath, and self-affirmations all directly impact emotional regulation and play a huge role in the development of self-image via self-awareness, self-confidence, and self-determination.

Tip: If you would like to test the power of visualization as a separate strategy from the MBCC, take some time every day to simply imagine an activity you want to improve. Maybe you want to be a better public speaker or a better basketball player. The activity doesn't matter. Take time every day for a week and visualize yourself performing that activity in perfect form from beginning to end. The length of time it will take depends on the activity you want to improve. You need to stick as close to the real length of time for that activity as possible. Make a note of your performance before and after you do this for a week to see if there is any improvement. Fadare et al., 2022 provided the following guidance for performing this exercise:

1. Be clear on your objective

2. Use more than just imagery

3. Execute in real-time

4. Practice continuously

5. Routinely visualize the outcome

"Energy is not something tangible and material that can be directly observed, but is, rather, defined by what it does, or could do, in its various forms."

- Ferri & Cimini, 2020

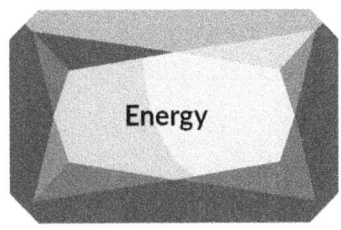

Infinity Stone #5

The fifth infinity stone may lose you if you are not open-minded. If you already understand and embrace the power of energy work, then you will instantly connect with this stone. However, if you have a hard time accepting the existence of this stone, you will not be able to experience the full transformative effect of the MBCC. The best way to describe the infinite presence of God is energy. Energy is all around us, within us, and in everything we see and encounter. The more we become in tune with our energy, the more sensitive we become to the energy of others and of the environment.

It's good we previously went over visualization because that is what we need to do for this section. Imagine people don't look like human beings. Rather, they look like bodies of energy.

Note: energy as I see it looks like light, so when I say imagine a body of energy, I'm suggesting a body of light. However, if you have a different idea for energy, go for it.

There is positive and negative energy all around us and within us. These energies within us are innate. This is proven in the instance of an infant who cannot yet talk and can barely mobilize, but who knows they shouldn't touch something, so they pause and look for approval. It's the mischievous/negative energy within that causes them to make the attempt to do what they already know they shouldn't do. Sometimes, people intend to make others smile, and sometimes, people aim to make others cry. It is what it is.

MIND AND BODY TRANSFORMATION

When we encounter people, we exchange energies. Sometimes, energies can be exchanged from a distance. Remember when you were a kid in school, and you licked out your tongue at a friend, and they took the whole class attempting to catch you looking at them so they could stick out their tongue at you? Do you remember how it felt when that friend caught you slipping, and you saw them out of the corner of your eye, stick their tongue out? That feeling was the transference of energy. We feel energy shift when people walk into a room. We exchange energies when we shake hands or embrace. We exchange energies when we kiss or make love. We absorb energy from people when they share their good or bad news with us. We release energy when we share our feelings with others, both in a positive and negative way.

David McManus talked about Reiki therapy which has become more widely explored by people seeking alternative healing options. Reiki was developed by Mikao Usui in Japan in the 1920s and is a form of alternative medicine. It is a "relaxing form of healing therapy that is applied through noninvasive, nonmanipulative gentle touch" (McManus 2017). In 2008, Dan Stone posited that Reiki practitioners believe "love is a universal life force energy" that flows through them to others both in person or at a distance and has the power to heal both the individual and the practitioner. Essentially, love is a healing energy that can be transferred back and forth through "conscious loving touch."

Between the years 2013 and 2017, I was a Supervisory Program Specialist in a 28-day residential substance-use and reentry facility for the federal government. During my time there, I witnessed individuals who were chronic marijuana users test positive for tetrahydrocannabinol (THC) weeks after being in the program and after already testing clean for all substances. This happened to residents that I knew were not using anything while in the facility. The reason this took place was because of how marijuana metabolizes in our bodies. Hansen et al., 2009 found that for chronic marijuana users, THC can be stored in the body's fatty tissues up to 77 days after their last usage. The storage of THC in the body's fat is so dense that after weeks of abstinence, an individual can experience "re-intoxication" as the drug reenters the bloodstream from a fatty hiding place (Hansen et al., 2009).

In the same way, marijuana finds places to hide in our bodies, so does negative energy. It disguises itself as a term we like to use called stress, and stress often collects in our neck, shoulders, and back. Sometimes, the energy hides internally in our organs and begins to impact how they function. Our brain, memory, digestive system, cardiovascular system, and immune systems are all adversely affected by stress, aka negative energy (Yaribeygi et al., 2017). Most notably, an immensely overlooked hiding place for negative energy is "unforgiveness" (Evans, 2021). In *Run to the Pain*, I talked about how a lack of forgiveness works in the back-office of our lives, causing us harm without us being aware of it. We will know if negative energy is lurking within us the second we are reminded of or face that person, place or event that hurt us. This is the roadblock that people frequently run into because they simply don't know how to forgive. Until the MBCC, which provides a path to releasing negative energy.

As we get older, we come to realize that our two most precious assets and currencies are our time and our energy. We start off with a percentage of energy each day, and that amount must be enough for everything and everyone we engage for the day, and we still need some for ourselves. My clients often forget that they need energy for themselves because they are uber-concerned about everyone else. We are ambassadors for our energy. Its potency, its positivity or negativity, and how much we give or absorb from others is our responsibility, and nobody else's.

The second we accept that nobody owes us anything and that the only people we owe are God and ourselves, we will be free to govern our energy with no reluctance, guilt, shame, or fear.

Tips: On Earth, there are either *Generators* or *Conductors*.

- **Generators** are (GIVERS), and they live to fulfill their purpose, which is to serve others. Generators are good people, but there are several pitfalls attached to this character trait:

1. They have a hard time saying "No."

2. Boundary setting is difficult for them.

3. They typically neglect themselves due to caring for others.

4. They are easier to manipulate and swindle.

5. They must learn to self-generate energy for themselves and not rely on others to be a source of energy. (The MBCC provides a tool for this.)

6. They need to build a social network of generators and minimize contact with conductors in their personal lives. It's quite likely their professional lives are dedicated to serving people.

• **Conductors** are (TAKERS) and spend more time asking people for favors than providing resources to people. See the below pitfalls to this character trait:

1. They tend to take a victim stance often.

2. They are generally emotionally shut off and burn social bridges.

3. They often operate from a place of lack, meaning because they use others as a crutch, they don't manage their resources well.

If a person attempts to transfer negative energy to you, the transference process is only successful if you accept the energy. Here is a quick story to illustrate this. One day, years ago, when I was working in downtown Washington DC, I was driving to work, and a woman cut me off in traffic. At that time, I had already mastered road rage, so I did not react. Although I had to slam on my brakes, I applied an anger management strategy and was able to instantly quell an emotional response. Right after hitting my brakes, I saw the driver look in her side-view mirror at me, and she stuck her hand out of the window with her middle finger up. That moment was reminiscent of the second grade, and it was as if my classmate was sticking her tongue out at me. However, at this time, I was a mature adult with an understanding of energy and protecting my peace. Again, I didn't respond. The driver then stuck her hand back out of the window with multiple middle finger flips. "Nope, I don't want your energy, and you can't have mine!" This is what I thought as I witnessed this random stranger attempt to offload her negative energy on me. So, then she started to hit her brakes in an attempt to make me hit mine. As you can see, when people fail to dump their energy on us, sometimes it makes them respond more erratically. At this time, I backed up to give her space so that she could get up the road. She then took the same left turn I needed to take. As I took the turn, I saw her pull over and begin to roll her window down so that she could stick her head out of the window and engage in a well-deserved venomous exchange of words/energies. For me, it was an opportunity to leave her sitting right there holding all that negativity. I like to call it emotional constipation when people have pent-up emotions that they don't know what to do with. I didn't even look over in her direction as I drove by. I believe to this day, that woman is still bitter due to her failed attempt to transfer her energy to me.

Note: Generators! Never be worried about conductors! If you tell a conductor "No," they will simply move on to the next person. So, be OK with your "No" and respond with a guilt-free "I don't have it, or I'm unavailable." Trust me, if the ground opens right where you are and people start falling in it, it will be the generators who die first. While I'm running towards the gaping hole in the ground to make sure people are safe, the conductors will be someplace on high ground, ensuring their survival. If a world-ending event takes place, it will be the conductors who repopulate the earth! There is no right or wrong in this. There is only what is true. Set your boundaries, be selective about your energy

distribution, and get comfortable with the word "No." Also, "I'm unavailable" works plenty!

"Stress is not what happens to you, but how you react to it."

- Hans Selye

Acute Stress Response (Fight or Flight)

Every outstanding meal has a secret ingredient! Since I'm a sauce man, I will call this the secret sauce. Think about a jumbo lump crab cake. It requires some form of binder, such as mayonnaise or breadcrumbs and eggs, to keep the meat together. In this way, the body's acute stress response, or more specifically, the sympathetic nervous system's hypothalamic-pituitary-adrenocortical (HPA) axis, is the binder that holds together the ingredients of the MBCC. This is where the magic happens, and we will discuss how this physiological response to stress plays a role in the application of the infinity stones and, ultimately, a transformational process.

When we hear about emotional regulation, anger management, or strategies to improve anxiety or depression, how many tools involve intentionally increasing our heart rate and/or putting ourselves in a stressful situation? Conversely, the prescription to address these challenges typically involves strategies such as cognitive reappraisal, meditation, and breath work, removing stressful stimuli from our lives, setting boundaries, and distancing ourselves from the catalysts of negative emotions (McRae & Gross 2020). Consequently, the lowering of blood pressure and stress is generally suggested to be a result of cutting out burdensome and emotionally agitating people and activities. Likewise, when we think of self-care, we usually think of rest and relaxation, massages, vacations, and leisure activities. Self-care is rarely if ever, associated with placing ourselves in the exact situations that lead to us feeling stressed and overwhelmed.

This is undoubtedly what makes the cheat code unique. The MBCC requires us to trigger our body's acute stress response. Keep in mind that stress is not always negative. As we discussed earlier, our perception of any given situation is how we will define the body's physiological response. Remember when my father and I were in the car as it spun out in the middle of the street? That event initiated the same acute stress response for us both. However, I perceived the event as exciting and fun, while on the other hand, my father was completely terrified. Hans Selye defined stress this way as "the nonspecific response of the body to any demand, whether it is caused by, or results in, pleasant or unpleasant conditions" (Tan & Yip, 2018). In 1971, Levi was the first to discuss the differences in stress and referred to them as positive or negative. Shortly after that, Hans Selye renamed the two physiological responses distress and eustress. Distress is associated with negative and unpleasant emotions, while eustress is germane to positive emotions (Szabo, Tache, & Somogyi, 2012). The fact that both positive and negative events trigger the body's acute stress response is significant. It's almost as significant as the fact that we control whether an event is perceived as positive or negative. Yet, the thing to remember is our perceptions can be manipulated! This is important because the MBCC is an activity in perception manipulation.

Now let's look at the physiological process of the acute stress response and see how it is relevant to the MBCC. Remember, in our earlier discussion on the vagus nerve, we talked about the central and peripheral nervous systems. To take it a step further, the peripheral nervous system (PNS), which houses the processing for the acute stress response, can be broken down into several components. The autonomic nervous system (ANS), a branch of the PNS, is comprised of the sympathetic nervous system (SNS), the parasympathetic nervous system (PRNS) and the enteric nervous system (ENS). The SNS initiates the body's fight or flight response, while the PRNS regulates the vagus nerve and sends communication back and forth between the brain and gut (Waxenbaum et al., 2023). When a threat to our lives happens, depending on the magnitude of the threat, our bodies will respond one of two ways. You have heard stories of a mother picking up a car that has her child trapped or fighting off a wild animal to protect her child. Under imminent life or death circumstances, the sympathomedullary pathway (SAM-p) is activated. "SAM-p releases catecholamines that modulate an immediate "fight or flight" response which optimize bodily functions for behavioral management of the stressor" (Caplin et al., 2021). In other words, an immediate Incredible Hulk response is triggered. However, the HPA axis, which is the focus of this book and the MBCC, "activates a longer transient hormonal cascade that terminates with the release of glucocorticoids (cortisol in humans) from the adrenal cortex" (Caplin et al., 2021). This is a built up Hulk response.

The following is an illustration of how the SNS and PRNS work in symphony to execute the body's acute stress response. It also demonstrates the process of the HPA Axis. Now, imagine walking to your car in a parking lot and seeing a masked person running towards you with a gun pointed in your direction. There are exceptions to the rule, but generally, there is a step-by-step process that takes place at this moment:

1. There is a split second taken for an "observation response." The hairs on the skin stand erect, and at this moment, the locus coeruleus releases norepinephrine (NE), activating the SNS. The paraventricular nucleus of the **hypothalamus** (first leg of the HPA axis) then produces corticotropin-releasing hormone (CRH). Here is where we look to escape/flight.[3]

2. While the heart rate accelerates and blood pressure rises, the **anterior pituitary gland** (the second leg of the HPA axis) induces proopiomelanocortin, a prohormone/polyprotein that, after synthesis, is cleaved to produce several distinct polypeptides. One

---

[3] (Heusch & Thämer, 1984; Fritz, et al., 2008; Furness, 2009; Rea, 2014; Karemaker, 2017; Morris, et al., 2020; Ridder et al., 2023; Waxenbaum et al., JA, 2023)

peptide in particular, adrenocorticotropin hormone (ACTH), triggers the next step in the stress response, and another is beta-endorphin, a pain suppressant. At this point, somatosensory perception and awareness are dampened, and you would not feel the effects of being hit or wounded. Your mouth would also become dry.

3. Muscles start to shiver. The SNS then triggers a process allowing for the reorganization of the blood supply. Vasoconstriction of peripheral vessels takes place redirecting blood flow from certain organs and concentrating it in the heart and other muscles. This also decreases the likelihood of blood loss after injury. Blood pressure subsequently rises due to increased cardiac output. The **adrenal cortex** (third leg of the HPA axis) then releases cortisol, which is known as the body's stress hormone. [4]

---

[4] (Heusch & Thämer, 1984; Fritz, et al., 2008; Furness, 2009; Rea, 2014; Karemaker, 2017; Morris, et al., 2020; Ridder et al., 2023; Waxenbaum et al., JA, 2023)

4. At this point, your body would be ready to fight if necessary.

5. As we discussed during the section on vagal tone and breathing, faster and deeper breathing is required to facilitate oxygenation of the organs and muscles. This would lead to increased perspiration, which cools the body down.

6. Hands become moist to assist with improved grip to better handle things during a fight or escape attempt.

7. The PRNS shuts down activities of the body that are not acutely needed during the stress response, such as digestion and bowel mobility. In instances where a stressful event is anticipated, the PRNS will attempt to eliminate urine and bowel from the body prior to the event, to make you lighter on your feet for war.

(Heusch & Thämer, 1984; Fritz, et al., 2008; Furness, 2009; Rea, 2014; Karemaker, 2017; Morris, et al., 2020; Ridder et al., 2023; Waxenbaum et al., JA, 2023)

The above stress response is referred to as the "bottom-up" response to stress. This primitive response allows for our emotions to dictate our behavior. Sometimes, we need our instincts to simply kick in and save our lives. Conversely, the "top-down" response to a traumatic event is when we maintain command of our "thinking brain." (Wang, Vlemincx, et al., 2022). Essentially, we keep our frontal lobe/pre-frontal cortex "online," stop our amygdala from taking over, and redirect our energy to remaining calm and problem-solving. The secret sauce of the MBCC is intentionally activating the acute stress response and taking the body through the HPA axis process so that we can enter a simulation mode, and essentially master the top-down response.

Note: The MBCC does not require you to already be in above-average physical health. Some people reading this book may be obese, out of shape, or never exercised a day in their lives. The MBCC meets you at your current state of physical conditioning.

For some people, walking up a flight of steps may cause their heart rate to increase significantly. While it may take me to sprint at top speed to reach 170-180 heartbeats per minute, it may take others a walk to the mailbox. In any event, we can practice the MBCC at any point when our RSA requires us to take deep breaths to regulate our breathing. At that point, our bodies may be triggering the HPA axis, and we have reached the sweet spot to practice the strategy.

When you think of deep breaths, think of them as opportunities!

Cross-Stressor Adaptation Hypotheses

Let's rewind the tape and go back to the beginning when I discovered the secret sauce to the MBCC. Once I stumbled on the vagus nerve and its role in our emotional health, I began to research, and it led me to vagal tone and the HPA Axis. Breadcrumbs then guided me to research by Theresa Kestly, who studied the acute stress response and used play therapy to discover if the body's alarm response can be regulated and adjusted to positive instead of negative. During her research, she found that the HPA Axis is activated during play (Kestly, 2016). I then sought to answer the question, "Does exercise prompt the same physiological response as the acute stress response? In 2008, Stranahan, Lee, and Mattson explored this question and found that due to its demand for energy, running recruits systems involved with the body's "fight or flight"/acute stress response. Running has been associated with heightened pituitary activity and elevated levels of ACTH, which suggests increased functioning of the HPA axis. Running, like other stressors, also activates the sympathetic nervous system, resulting in the HPA axis and glucocorticoid production. Stranahan et al. followed the path of the neuroendocrine stress axis/ HPA axis in both males and females while exercising and found the following progression of physiological responses:

1. The amygdala sends messages to the paraventricular nucleus of the **hypothalamus**.

2. The hypothalamus then releases corticotropin-releasing hormone (CRH).

3. The anterior **pituitary** produces adrenocorticotropin hormone (ACTH).

4. ACTH signals the **adrenal gland** to release glucocorticoids Cortisol (Stranahan, et al., 2008).

This was the light bulb moment for me. I thought, "Well, if our bodies react to exercise and play the same way they do when we are in fear for our lives, then there must be some correlation between physically fit people, emotional intelligence, and an ability to manage anger and emotions." Of course, I thought I was the only person who was asking this question until I saw that in 1996,

Sothmann et al. explored the cross-stressor adaptation hypotheses. They sought to find out if exercise training could modify the physiological stress response to "nonexercised stressors." In other words, does exercise training also train people to manage stressors such as anxiety, anger, or frustration? In theory, this hypothesis would track since as we previously discussed, the strength and condition of one's vagal tone are parallel to one's ability to regulate emotions, and we just discussed how exercise and play trigger the HPA axis (Sothmann et al., 1996; Stranahan, et al., 2008; Kestly, 2016; Messerli-Bürgy, N., et al., 2020).

I thought for sure that Sothmann and company were on to something big and would confirm some promising results. Remarkably, their findings suggested that there was no correlation between physically fit people and emotional regulation, emotional intelligence, or an ability to effectively handle life stressors.

Note: *Emotional regulation* is one's ability to manage/control his/her feelings. Basically, an ability to manage the intensity of emotions such as anger during triggering moments, or anxiety while handling an overwhelming experience. *Emotional intelligence* is a heightened sense of self-awareness and the ability to effectively select behavioral responses at the most appropriate times, places, and with the appropriate people in accordance with a desired emotional outcome. When I discovered Sothmann's research, I thought, "Well, this makes sense because otherwise, how would we explain the professional athletes who lost their careers for assaulting women on elevators, sexually assaulting women, or murdering people and then committing suicide? How would we account for the multitude of athletes who emotionally unravel before our eyes on courts, fields, or behind microphones during interviews around the world on a daily basis?" Hence, I thought I hit a roadblock in my theory until I realized the likely reason for those findings back in 1996. There is a fundamental disconnect between athletes training for a sporting event and training that is required for emotional regulation, and *intentionality* is required to make the connection.

So, I kept digging and found several others who researched the cross-stressor adaptation hypothesis, and a few studies drawing a correlation between physical fitness and endocrine stress reactivity connected to nonexercised stressors (Klaperski et al., 2014; Rimmele et al., 2007, 2009)). Studies of the cross-stress adaptation hypotheses commonly used the levels of "free" or unbound cortisol in saliva, or "salivary free cortisol," to determine if the HPA axis initiated the acute stress response and to what level of intensity (Caplin et al., 2021; Puterman et al., 2012; Rimmele et al., 2009; Rimmele et al., 2007; Traustadóttir et al., 2005; Wunsch et al., 2019). In addition to salivary-free cortisol, heart rate (HR) and heart rate variability (HRV) have been used as measurements of stress. To elicit psychological stress in participants, researchers of the cross-stress adaptation hypotheses have been using the Trier Social Stress Test for Groups (TSST-G), a "standardized protocol for inducing psychosocial stress" (Klaperski et al., 2014; Von Dawans et al., 2011).

Sandra Klaperski and her team tested 149 healthy men in a 12-week exercise training and used salivary-free cortisol, HR, and HRV as measurements to determine if the exercise training they provided improved the participants' acute stress response to activities that were designed to generate psychological stress. The TSST-G was used to ignite psychological stress in the participants (Von Dawans et al., 2011). The test required the participants to perform mock job interviews, solve mathematical problems, and give public speeches. Their results found a correlation between physical fitness and emotional regulation.

Even though I previously mentioned the MBCC meets you at your level of physical fitness, you may still be asking yourself, especially if you're not physically fit or actively exercising, "What about those people who are out of shape and couldn't even tell you what the inside of a gym looks like...Can those people use the MBCC knowing the requirement for the physical fitness infinity stone?" That's a great question and I'm grateful for your inquiry. Keep in mind that the critical purpose of the physical fitness infinity stone is to access the body's acute stress response and the HPA axis. For people with low levels of physical fitness, it takes less work for them to trigger the body's acute stress response compared to those who are physically fit. If by the time you walk to your bedroom you have been sweating, and your heart rate has increased enough to stimulate the production of CRH and ACTH, then you have a critical moment where you can practice the MBCC right in your bedroom.

Remember to take advantage of every opportunity to breathe! In 2021, Caplin et al. sought to uncover if the intensity of exercise had any influence on the intensity of psychological stress one is capable of managing. Meaning do you have to be an elite athlete to experience the intended emotional regulatory effects of exercise? The short answer is No, you don't have to be a superior athlete or be in good shape at all. Caplin et al. studied Eighty-three healthy men who were "randomly assigned to exercise on a treadmill at either 30%, 50% or 70% of their heart rate reserve (HRR) for 30 min." What they found is the level of exercise intensity correlated with how much psychological stress participants could handle and the speed of their recovery (Caplin et al., 2021). These findings suggest that the emotional regulatory effects of exercise will meet you at your level of physical fitness. In other words, the more intense you can exercise, the more psychological stress you can train yourself to handle. Conversely, this does not suggest that exercises of low to moderate intensity do not provide any benefit. Rather, it simply means low to moderate exercise provides a benefit in accordance with the intensity of the exercise. To access the HPA axis, you have to move at the intensity level of at least a brisk walk (Caplin et al., 2021). However, even that level of intensity will give you the opportunity to practice the MBCC. This is important for those of you who are currently out of shape and still wish to apply the MBCC. Allow the strategy to meet you where you are.

So, let's connect the dots. In previous studies, researchers used a standardized test to elicit psychological stress, that was not explicit to the personal trauma or life stressors of the participants. Researchers have been able to draw a connection between physical fitness and emotional regulation, but the MBCC takes this finding a step further and gives you a method to regulate specific emotions related to distinct people, places, or events. I played basketball and football and ran track for organizations throughout my youth and on a collegiate level. In all my years of training for sports, my consistent goal was to get faster, stronger, or better in that sport. I wanted to beat my previous time, my previous max lift, or beat the guy next to me.

Never in my sports training did I think, "I want to beat my anger!," "I want to be more patient!" or "I need to release this pressure!" Every year of high school when football season ended and track season began, I knew my body was going to undertake a different level of conditioning. Football required tough physical conditioning, but with respect to cardiovascular conditioning, it did not compare to running track. I remember gasping for air after runs, hands on my knees, and my coach telling me, "The air is up top!" This meant I needed to stand up and keep walking while catching my breath. All those massive breaths I took that were strengthening my respiratory sinus arrhythmia, my heart muscle, and my vagal tone were dedicated solely to becoming a better athlete and not a better overall person.

Transformation Simulation

What if I took advantage of those moments when my body entered the acute stress response and initiated the HPA axis? Those moments when my body was precisely in the physiological state that it would be in if I were fighting or running for my life. Why can't people use those moments to train for life stressors and not just improve cardiovascular strength? What if people realized that these moments, with each breath, were an opportunity to transform who they were?

When I think of a *simulation*, I think of an environment that places a person in a scenario that feels as close to a real-world experience as possible. The military uses staged grounds that resemble actual battlefields, terrain, potential threats, and enemy forces to train soldiers as if they are in a real battle (Stergiou et al.,

2023). Can you imagine if soldiers waited until it was time for war to start practicing for it? Simulations have been used for decades to train people in various careers including aviation, nursing and healthcare professionals, law enforcement, and education (Baarspul, 1990; Fuentes-García, 2021; Koukourikos et al., 2021; Rasteiro, 2023; Stergiou et al., 2023).

This section is not aimed at arguing the validity or effectiveness of simulations. However, its purpose is to highlight the very real opportunity we possess to train for the war we all wage against emotional dysregulation, suppressed disappointment, shame and guilt, devalued self-image, counterproductive thinking, and maladaptive behavior. We have a genuine chance, with every inspiration of oxygen, to also breathe in the version of us we aspire to be and, with every expiration, release the version of us that does not best represent us. This is the missing link in the cross-stressor adaptation hypotheses. When our hearts are beating at 150 beats per minute, and we have entered the acute stress response, we are given the opportunity to train ourselves to calm down with controlled diaphragmatic breathing, and that is the moment we must be intentional about what we are visualizing, self-affirming and what energy we are pulling in and pushing out with every breath.

Crisis Thinking

One of the complaints I receive from clients who attempt to implement the MBCC during exercise is that it is extremely challenging to concentrate on the emotions you are breathing in and out when you're busy attempting to catch your breath. If you're in the gym and on a treadmill for example, you must manage several stimuli at the same time while attempting to think critically. You may be listening to music, the television is on, there are people in the gym, you're attempting to remain coordinated so you don't fall off the exercise equipment, you are physically exerting yourself, and you are attempting to catch your breath, which can be extremely difficult when you are not in good cardiovascular strength. This requires elite concentration, and when you first attempt this, it may feel overwhelming. That is the point of this stage of the cheat code.

Think about when you are in a crisis. When you are facing a huge argument, suffering a panic attack, or attempting to juggle the many responsibilities of being an adult, is it a peaceful, orderly, and well-organized time in your life? I can answer that for you! NO! All hell is breaking loose in those moments! These are the moments when your life is seemingly falling apart when people tend to shut down, stick their heads in the sand, and isolate themselves from the world. These are the moments when people say they couldn't think or didn't want to think. And it is for these reasons we must train ourselves to do the very thing we love to avoid in a crisis…THINK! The MBCC conditions us to think critically in the middle of chaos.

"We can learn to restrain our aggressive dispositions, be led not to think of others as sources of displeasure, and turn our thoughts away from aggression-promoting ideas."

- Berkowitz, 1983

The Mind & Body Cheat Code (MBCC)

(The Infinity Gauntlet)

The MBCC is a psychophysiological regulatory exercise that combines physical fitness, breath work, self-affirmations, visualization, and energy work to provide a moment for self-transformation. This exercise is a PROACTIVE approach to training for current and future real-life events. I stressed proactive because we are conditioned in American society to be reactive. Our healthcare system doesn't provide key medications or preventative examinations until <u>after</u> we show signs and symptoms of an illness or until <u>after</u> we reach a certain age. People don't typically come to therapy until <u>after</u> they are experiencing emotional difficulties or problems in their relationships. However, the reality is for most experiences we have in life, we earned the outcomes. This means, unbeknown to us, we have been unintentionally proactive about the results we have received and will receive in life. Think about it. Aside from hereditary factors outside of our control, we don't just wake up with hypertension or high cholesterol. We don't just catch type II diabetes like it's a common cold. The same goes for how we manage our emotions, how we face conflicts in our lives, how we treat relationships or process grief, and how we heal from trauma or value ourselves. We don't just wake up one day with a negative view of ourselves, a distrust for others, or an emotional unavailability. These approaches to life's circumstances were cultivated over time. Our core beliefs are a culmination of how we have experienced the world since birth, so when it comes to transforming ourselves into a better version, it will take intentional, proactive, and consistent effort.

How does this translate to real life? Stop waiting until you're in the middle of a crisis or during its aftermath to practice breathing strategies or the tools you have learned for emotional regulation. Don't wait until your life is falling apart before you decide to make a change! Start thinking multiple moves ahead and be careful with "taking life one day at a time" thinking! Reupholster your thinking and your approach to managing your emotions and behaviors.

In the 1980's, I remember spending time with my grandparents during the summer months. My grandfather, who is 89 years old, would expend a great amount of effort reupholstering furniture. I watched him undo the stitching of a chair, remove the outer covering made of fabric or old leather, replace the inner cushions with fresh and firm stuffing, and stitch new material on the chair, essentially making it a new piece of furniture. In the same way those couches and chairs were torn down and rebuilt, we must tear down our antiquated and failed approaches to emotional and behavioral change, and replace them with a pioneering, weather-tested, and proactive approach. To do this, you must accept your way as inadequate and become intentional about practicing something unfamiliar, uncomfortable, and fresh.

I use the MBCC daily, and aside from my *Why*, it is the primary reason I remain consistent with exercise. I don't exercise every day to get stronger or to look good in clothes. That's a bonus. I exercise for the proactive opportunity to train for war against the old and lesser version of myself. The version of myself who is quick to anger, impatient, anxious, fearful, depressed, lazy, and shifty. I practice the MBCC to become a man of patience, balance, excellence, faith, peace, confidence, and integrity.

Note: I have no doubt that some of you who are reading this do not have a problem with getting started with a self-care routine or remaining consistent. For you, all you require are the steps to the cheat code, and you will simply apply them to your daily regimen. If that's you, I salute you! However, trust me, for every one of you, there are no less than fifty others who are struggling and need to reinvent themselves while getting this strategy underway.

Cheat Code/My Daily Routine

1. I prioritize myself <u>first</u> in the morning. It's mandatory, just like brushing my teeth or washing up. I get my day started properly by directing my intentions, emotions, and energy. Also, "cortisol has a circadian rhythm in which levels dramatically decrease in the morning, and are relatively stable in the afternoon" (Dickerson, & Kemeny, 2004). This suggests that I have the ability to manage my emotions more effectively by implementing a morning exercise routine.

2. It is a requirement to move. It can start as stretching until you get yourself conditioned to moving and/or getting out of the house. Ideally, you will do a form of high-intensity interval training (HIIT). In doing so, you will elevate your heart rate, which is a requirement to activate the body's acute stress response. I do a sprint and walk rotation for about 15 minutes, followed by about 10 minutes of stretching on most days, but on other days, it might be burpees, jumping rope, or box jumps. According to Dickerson & Kemeny, 21-40 minutes of exercise is a sweet spot for accessing the HPA axis.

3. I sprint for 30 seconds and then walk for one minute and thirty seconds. During the walk, time is where the magic happens. This can be any exercise where you increase the resistance for a period to get your heart rate elevated, and then you slow the pace enough to focus on breathing and calming down.

4. Throughout the entire exercise, I am mindful of my breathing. There are moments when you are attempting to catch your breath where diaphragmatic breathing is used to take in as much oxygen as possible. However, there is a strategy for breathing that will help maximize oxygen intake while also intentionally lowering the heart rate. When we inhale, the heart rate increases, and when we exhale, the heart rate deescalates. So, when we are catching our breath, if we are aggressively taking large breaths, we will not lower our heart rate as quicky as we would prefer. The objective will be to breathe in as calmly as possible, even when your heart rate is high. I have learned to take quick breaths and slowly exhale without forcing out the air, and this lowers my heart rate the fastest.

5. During this time of mindful breathing, I practice a strategy introduced by Golwitzer in 1999 called "implementation intentions." The purpose of implementation intentions is to "translate goal intentions into action." "Goal intentions can be

defined as the instructions that people give themselves to perform particular behaviors or to achieve certain desired outcomes" (Golwitzer, 1999). These are better known as "If, Then statements" (Łakuta, 2020). We speak to ourselves this way all the time, programming ourselves to achieve goals without even realizing it. "If she says one more thing to me, I will... or They got one more time to speak to me that way, and I'm gonna..." Does that sound familiar? Linking the if-part to the then-part produces automaticity, which means that when the specified situation is encountered, it triggers the desired response automatically. This is a form of self-training. Now let's transition this approach from one with counterproductive intent to one with good intent.

6. I also combine self-affirming implementation intentions with another technique called "mental contrasting." Mental contrasting takes place when a future positive desire or outcome is contrasted with our current reality which stands in the way (Cross & Sheffield,

2016). For example, if we currently feel anger towards someone, but we desire to feel love towards them, we must think about loving that person in the face of the anger we currently feel. Research suggests that combining both implementation intentions and mental contracting constitutes a "synergistic strategy for self-regulated behavior change" that has been shown to be more effective than either implementation intentions or mental contrasting alone (Wang, Wang, & Gai, 2021).

7. Each time a cycle of mindful breathing comes around (between intense intervals of exercise), a different intervention is deployed. I start with self-affirmations and committing to the version of myself I choose to be. This means breathing in a character trait I embrace, such as integrity, and breathing out a trait that I do not identify with, such as laziness. During the next cycle of mindful breathing, I breathe in the emotions that I choose to embrace for the day and breathe out those I choose to release.

During the next cycle, I breathe in the aspects of people who I have a problem with and breathe out the qualities of that person that I choose to forgive. (Sometimes it's forgiveness of self.)

8. During this time of large inhales and exhales, when I breathe in, I not only visualize the word I want to accept, but I bring my hands from an extended posture away from my boy and pull my hands inward. When I breathe out, I push my hands away from my body and I envision myself pushing the emotion away that I need to release... #Energywork

Infinity Stone #6

The principal goal of the inqubo is to provide an opportunity to Accept and Release. **Accepting and Releasing are the two most difficult things for people to do, and they are an absolute requirement for any change process.** When you think about any area of your life where you feel stuck, 100% of the time, you must accept something and release something else. There is no exception to this rule. The 5 elements of the cheat code are simply a means to an end. They are the journey to the proverbial "Acceptance and Release Infinity Stone." This stone is forged by the synthesis of all

5 stones. So, when I'm breathing out pressure, I'm releasing it, and when I'm breathing in peace, I'm accepting it. For some people, the acceptance and release process may have to do with accepting that a person will not change so that they can release themselves from the guilt attached to leaving that person.

- Examples of how I incorporate both implementation intentions and mental contrasting are listed below under the categories I am addressing for self-improvement, (this is what I say to myself as I breathe in and out, and the capitalized words are what I visually see in my mind; my personal self-affirmations). You can use the ones I developed for myself, but you are strongly encouraged to develop your own affirmations:

Emotional Regulation

(Visualize the words in CAPS getting bold as they come to you and fading away as they leave you.)

- If RAGE (hands push out with the exhale), then RELAX (hands pull in with the inhale).

- If CRAZY (hands push out with the exhale), then CALM (hands pull in with the inhale).

- If DEPRESSED (hands push out with the exhale), then GRATITUDE (hands pull in with the inhale).

- If FRUSTRATED (hands push out with the exhale), then PATIENCE (hands pull in with the inhale).

Mental Clarity

(Visualize the words in CAPS getting bold as they come to you and fading away as they leave you.)

- If PRESSURE (hands push out with the exhale), then PEACE (hands pull in with the inhale).

- If FOGGY (hands push out with the exhale), then CLARITY (hands pull in with the inhale).

Spirituality

(Visualize the words in CAPS getting bold as they come to you and fading away as they leave you.)

- If FEAR (hands push out with the exhale), then FAITH (hands pull in with the inhale).

Character

(Visualize the words in CAPS getting bold as they come to you and fading away as they leave you.)

- If QUIT (hands push out with the exhale), then GRIT (hands pull in with the inhale).

- If DOUBT (hands push out with the exhale), then COMPLETION (hands pull in with the inhale).

- If LESS (hands push out with the exhale), then BEST (hands pull in with the inhale).

- If WEAKNESS (hands push out with the exhale), then STRENGTH (hands pull in with the inhale).

- If PRIDE (hands push out with the exhale), then HUMBLE (hands pull in with the inhale).

- If MEDIOCRITY (hands push out with the exhale), then EXCELLENCE (hands pull in with the inhale).

- If LAZY (hands push out with the exhale), then INTEGRITY (hands pull in with the inhale).

Forgiveness

(Visualize the face of the person who violated you while watching the words come and go.)

- If ANGER (hands push out with the exhale), then EMBRACE (hands pull in with the inhale). (For those who you want to keep in your life.)

- If GUILT (hands push out with the exhale), then GRACE (hands pull in with the inhale.) (For those who you want to keep your life.)

- If PRIDE (hands push out with the exhale), then EMBRACE (hands pull in with the inhale.) (For those who you want to keep in your life.)

- If ANGER (hands push out with the exhale), then FREE (hands pull in with the inhale). (For those who you want to remove your life.)

- If PRIDE (hands push out with the exhale), then FREE (hands pull in with the inhale.) (For those who you want to remove your life.)

- If GUILT (hands push out with the exhale), then FREE (hands pull in with the inhale.) (For those who you want to remove your life.)

Your evening routine dictates your morning routine. If you struggle to get up early to prioritize yourself, it could be because you need to take your butt to bed!

By doing this process at least Monday-Friday for the last five years, I have experienced improved vagal tone, improved emotional regulation, great physical health results, and a vastly improved sense of self-worth, which is reinforced by self-trust and simply doing what I say I'm going to do. I have used the above affirmations to train for potential conflicts so that I was able to be in close proximity with people who previously disrespected me. I literally saw the person's face in my mind dozens of times before I was physically in their presence. This has been a game-changer! As previously mentioned, this approach is the cheat code because it ties in five bodies of research, all designed to improve emotional regulation, cognitive functioning, and improved self-identity, and this is done simultaneously. In addition, there is an array of physical health benefits including improved mood, regulated blood pressure, improved immune system, efficient digestive system, and better overall quality of life. Essentially, the process addresses all of our organizational health departments: Mental, physical, emotional, spiritual, and social.

With Dr. E's Mind & Body Cheat Code, not only are you conditioning your heart and body physically, but you're conditioning the physiological aspect of your body's acute stress response to broaden the body's tool kit and menu of options for responding during times of anger, frustration, anxiety, and panic. Conditioning the automaticity of a more productive, calm, and rational response during these moments. Not only are you training yourself to have more healthy and prosocial responses, but you are also being proactive in preparing yourself for handling the daily pressure of life; as well as preparing your mind for future interactions with people you may have a problem with. Direct your day or be an extra in someone else's movie. This is why the inqubo must be done first thing in the morning.

You also get to affirm who you are. There is nothing more impactful in our lives than our self-identity. Our self-identity, or self-image, dictates our self-value and worth, our standards, our integrity and trustworthiness, our propensity for violence and ratchet behavior... everything. During the time we spend with the MBCC, we get to commit and recommit to the version of ourselves we want to be. Identify who you are and who you want to be. That commitment comes before all others.

When you break your commitment to someone else, no matter the commitment, you may be dishonoring that person or relationship, but you are honoring your commitment to your truest self-identity. Is that the identity you want to embrace?

The MBCC provides the much-needed opportunity to release negative energy and practice forgiveness. As mentioned in *Run to the Pain*, "Forgiveness is the release of negative energy directed towards an event or person" (Evans, 2021). Holding on to negative energy in the form of anger because we believe it's a form of accountability, is a mistake. In that instance, we are only holding ourselves accountable for the internal damage done by harboring negative emotions/stress. Finally, the MBCC offers a chance for us to pour into ourselves before anyone else. This sounds like a foreign language to many, especially mothers. By the way, my clients who are mothers struggle with prioritizing themselves at all, not to mention putting themselves even closer to the top of the priority list. For those of us who are givers, we have a hard time prioritizing ourselves and creating space to receive. Since givers are typically surrounded by takers, we must learn how to self-generate energy, and that looks like pouring into ourselves first. This way, we can serve others with a guilt-free conscience. Ironically, some people have been so programmed to give to everyone else that they feel guilty doing it for themselves. If this is you, I pray that you receive this message and give yourselves permission to be the best version of yourself, not just for you but for those you love as well. This looks like sticking to your daily routine and plugging things and people in as needed or if they fit.

Instead of revolving your life around everything and everyone, revolve everything and everyone around your life.

Note: If you cannot trust yourself, you are not a trustworthy person, which impacts your self-image and how others view you. Commit to Dr. E's method for the next 30 days and watch the changes happen in your life. Most importantly, make note of how much more you respect yourself and demand respect from others through your example.

The Mind & Body Cheat Code is a tool that provides us with a method to do the following:

- Reinvent yourself and commit/recommit to self

- Become the best version of yourself

- Change old maladaptive and unproductive behaviors

- Manage anger and emotions

- Manage anxiety proactively

- Address mental, physical, emotional, and spiritual health departments simultaneously

- Increase self-discipline

- Learn to prioritize yourself first

- Learn to let go and forgive

"Until you identify your self-care as God-care, and crystalize it as THE TOP priority, you will remain in a perpetual state of imbalance!"

- Dr Robert Evans, III

Dr. E's Research Study

Title

The Impact of Dr. E's Mind & Body Cheat Code on Grief and Anger Amongst Collegiate Level Athletes

Statement of the Problem

It is well-researched and known that exercise, breath work, self-affirmations, visualization, and energy work all have been used as tools for physical and emotional healing and self-improvement and have positive influences on various aspects of a person's organizational health. Organizational health is defined as the inclusivity of an individual's physical, mental, emotional, spiritual, and social health departments. If individually practiced, each one of these tools has been shown to improve emotional regulation, cognitive functioning, and behavioral outcomes. Additionally, with the exception of exercise, all of the tools have helped people to improve areas of their lives without intense stimulation of the vagus nerve and in the absence of accessing the body's acute stress response. We know the vagus nerve and vagal tone directly influence emotional regulation. We also have seen research suggesting that athletes who have been conditioning their cardiovascular strength have also been conditioning themselves to manage life stressors better. Prior research supports a correlation between physical fitness and emotional regulation and recovery from emotional strain. However, the consistent theme amongst previous research on the cross-stressor adaptation hypotheses is that the psychological stress used in the studies has been generic and did not apply to the specific and personal challenges of the research participants. Moreover, we know that the Mind & Body Cheat Code (MBCC) is intended to target an individual's personal and distinct emotional, psychological, and behavioral challenges. Additionally, the MBCC combines all of the aforementioned tools while also stimulating the vagus nerve, building vagal tone, and accessing the body's acute stress responses along with the HPA axis.

What has yet to be researched, aside from Dr. E's personal experience and the purported experiences of his clients, is the impact of the MBCC on successfully eliminating undesired thinking, emotions, and behavior. The MBCC is asserted to be a "one-stop shop," essentially providing a therapeutic method to change and transform anything a person desires about themselves. This assertion must be tested!

Research Design

In 2014, Sandra Klaperski and colleagues set out to test the cross-stressor adaptation hypotheses and were able to draw a correlation between physical fitness and emotional regulation, suggesting that the more fit a person is, the more they are capable of mitigating psychological stress. They applied commonly used measurements amongst many other researchers who tested the validity of the cross-stressor adaptation hypotheses, such as saliva testing, heart rate and heart rate variability testing, and the use of the Trier Social Stress Test (TSST). They broke up the participants into three groups and used an analysis of variance (ANOVA) for statistical analysis. This study would use a similar design but seek to measure more specific outcomes. Additionally, the TSST would be modified so that instead of generic stimuli, explicit points of grief and anxiety identified by the participants would be used to induce psychological stress (Klaperski et al., 2014).

Target Population and Participant Selection

While the MBCC can help anyone who uses it, it does require an individual to trigger their acute stress response, which means they need to be at a level of physical fitness that provides them the ability to perform some level of exercise. While there needs to be research that assesses the impact of the MBCC for individuals on all levels of physical fitness, this study would start with participants who have already mastered the challenges of consistency with respect to exercise and self-care. Thus, collegiate-level athletes would be used as participants. Many college athletes are on scholarship and are committed to their fitness goals. The study would be presented to the athletic department and the social sciences departments of local colleges to gain support to use their scholar-athletes. The athletes can be incentivized to participate by being given extra credit for classes that coincide with the research. Athletes from all the sports on the campuses would be solicited. The goal would be to garner as many participants as possible, so three to four schools would be involved.

Research Questions

Question 1: Is there a predictive relationship between effective grief management and the mind & body cheat code?

Question 2: Is there a predictive relationship between specific anxiety and the mind & body cheat code?

Research Hypotheses

Hypothesis 1:

There will be a statistically significant predictive relationship between effective grief management and the mind & body cheat code.

Hypothesis 2:

There will be a statistically significant predictive relationship between specific anxiety and the mind & body cheat code.

Instruments

1. To capture Salivary Free Cortisol: A Saliva Sampling Device (Salivette; Sarstedt, Germany)

2. To measure Heart Rate (HR) and Heart Rate Variability (HRV): A wireless chest heart rate transmitter with a wrist monitor recorder (Polar RS800CX, Polar Electro, Finland)

3. 24-hour ambulatory blood pressure (BP) monitor (Ensari et al., 2020).

4. Ecological momentary assessment (EMA) of self-reported anxiety levels (Ensari et al., 2020).

5. To induce psychological stress: Modified version of the standardized Trier Social Stress Test (TSST). Participants will be required to visualize pre-identified points of anxiety or grief while performing the exercise and breathing activities.

6. Specific anxiety questionnaire. The anxiety questionnaire would ask the participants to identify a person, event, or activity that makes them anxious, worried, or afraid.

7. Specific grief questionnaire: A questionnaire asking the participants to identify a person they are estranged from. Someone who they care about or once cared about and who they feel anger, resentment, or a negative emotion towards. If it's not anger or resentment, they can identify their feeling directed towards that person.

Definition of Terms

• Mind & Body Cheat Code (MBCC): This is the strategy that entails performing the exercise, breath work, self-affirmations in the form of implementation intentions and mental contrasting, visualization, and energy work simultaneously.

• Grief: For this study, it is defined as anger, resentment, or negative emotion directed towards a person or event.

• Specific Anxiety: For this study, it is defined as worry or fear displayed by increased heart rate and self-report related to a person, event, or activity.

Procedures

In theory, the MBCC can be used to transform anything about a person. However, this study would start with grief and anxiety directed towards a specific person or event because these are common challenges reported by my clients. Participants would be given both the specific anxiety and the grief questionnaires to determine if they qualify for the study. They would need to identify on at least one of the questionnaires that they experience an intense negative emotion related to a person, place, or event. This would divide them into either a grief group or an anxiety group. Of those who qualify for the study, all of them would be used regardless of whether they identified as having grief or anxiety. If they identified trauma on both questionnaires, an attempt would be made to keep the groups of participants even.

1. Each of the participants would undergo an initial face-to-face interview. During the interview, the participants would be asked to

describe in as much detail as possible what took place that resulted in them having negative emotions, as indicated on their questionnaires.

2. During the interview, they would be connected to both the BP and HR monitors to measure their blood pressure and heart rates during the interview. The readings from both instruments would be recorded at the beginning of the interview, during the interview, and at the end to see if there is any fluctuation in blood pressure and heart rate while talking about their trauma.

3. Saliva samples would be taken prior to the interview and at the end of the interview.

4. After the interview, the participants would be given a series of quick training/demonstrations detailing how to incorporate the MBCC during their exercise/physical training routines.

5. They would receive a tutorial on self-affirmations, including implementation intentions and mental contrasting.

6. They would be shown how to practice diaphragmatic breathing in between exercise sets when they are attempting to catch their breath. This is the moment their body has entered the acute stress response and the HPA axis. This is the moment they need to control their breathing, visualize the person, event, or activity that they have a negative emotion towards, start saying the appropriate if-then statements that apply to their situation, and use the appropriate hand motions to pull and push energy. (Modified TSST)

7. The participants would then be given instructions to perform the MBCC during their normal exercise routines. Both the grief and anxiety groups would be divided into thirds. One-third of the group would be instructed to do the MBCC with exercise 3 days per week, one-third 5 days per week, and the other third 7 days per week. This is a total of 6 groups. All the groups would be required to use the MBCC for 30 days. This means of the 30 days, one group

would have a total of 12 days using the MBCC, one group a total of 20 days, and the other group 30 days.

8. After 30 days of using the MBCC with exercise, the participants would return for another interview requiring them to express the same story pertaining to the person or event that generated negative emotions. They would be asked to imagine the event and really take themselves back to it. At this time, they would again be connected to the BP and HR monitors. Saliva samples would once again be taken before and after the interviews. The results would be recorded to represent the beginning of the interview, during the interview and at the end.

9. The results of both the pre-and post-interviews would be analyzed to determine if there were any significant differences in the participant's blood pressure and heart rates while recalling and expressing their traumatic scenarios.

10. From there, any differences in the results for the six groups will also be analyzed and discussed.

11. At the end of the post-interview, participants would be given the EMA scale and the grief and specific anxiety questionnaires to see if they self-report any changes in how they feel about their identified trauma. Their self-report, along with the results of their BP and HR evaluations, would then be analyzed and discussed.

12. As a follow-up to this study, I would use a similar design and break the groups up so that some participants use all of the infinity stones during their exercise and compare them to groups who only use one or two stones but not all of them. This would be analyzed to see if any particular combination of stones works better than the others.

Conclusion

I would love for someone to take on this research and use this design or one they feel is better. I know this strategy works because

I use it, and it has come through for me in many ways. I would love for others to get a taste of the magic and spread the good news like it's the second coming! I always say that even if my thoughts just impact one person, I'm happy and have succeeded in my mission to change lives. With that said, go be that one! I promise you won't regret it! And you already know how I feel about my word!

"While MOST are coming up with excuses, complaining, pontificating on politics, debating who is the greatest, and waiting for someone else to decide their fate, there are those of us getting it done, seizing opportunities, leading the charge, becoming the greatest versions of ourselves, who are the subjects of debates and making power moves!"

- Dr. Robert L Evans, III

Acknowledgments

God

Thank you, God, for showing me your face! I appreciate our relationship and love the fact that whenever I have called on your name, Jesus, you have shown up and shown out! Thanks to you, I walk with confidence worry-free! Thank you for blessing me with passion, purpose, and the gifts to walk in it! With you as my *Why*, I maintain an unfailing consistency! You are the real cheat code!

Queen

You tell me all the time, "I see the divine in you." Well, I see the divine in you, on you, and all around you! I knew long ago you were one of God's angels! I'm thankful that you sit next to me in the car because I feel an extra layer of protection knowing you are one of God's starting five! I am forever grateful that our stars aligned! We make an amazing team, and I'm proud to have you as my life partner! Oh, and congratulations on your new book, *While I was waiting on God, He was waiting on Me*! Sold everywhere!

Children

You continue to be a source of motivation for me to remain a man of God, a man of integrity, and a man who leads by example! Thank you for being outstanding human beings and a ray of hope for our future as a human race.

Parents

You gave me the tools to be successful in this world. Your sacrifice has paid dividends!

Thank you!

Physical Health

Thank you for giving me a great opportunity to live a fulfilling life! I don't take you for granted for one second! You are not perfect, but I would choose you again and again, every day and all day!

Amen!

The Breath

You continue to provide me with an opportunity to become a better me! You sustain me and keep me balanced!

Thank you!

Vision

Thank you for allowing me to see my past mistakes so that I could learn from them! You allow me to see far beyond my current state of existence, and I'm happy to say that what I see is better than amazing! (Von voice)

Energy

You have not failed me yet! I have come to realize your value, and that's why I take the time to recharge you first thing. I don't allow everyone open access to you, and I don't freely accept others who do not share your frequency! You are priceless, and I will always treat you as such!

Self-Identity

I appreciate who you have been and who you are transforming into. You have made progress by leaps and bounds, and only Heaven is the limit for you! Stay consistent, continue to seek, remain open, and always be ready!

About the Author

Dr. Robert L. Evans, III is a culturally competent Psychologist, Licensed Clinical Professional Counselor, Clinically Certified Trauma Professional, and Master Addictions Counselor with over two decades of experience and a passion for helping individuals and families recognize thoughts and behaviors that hinder progress. He hopes when situations seem hopeless, and he believes when positive results appear unbelievable. His career has been dedicated to enlightening people with the keys to overcoming trauma, which is to forgive oneself and/or to forgive others. Dr. E. is the CEO of Empowerment Counseling & Training Services LLC and Integrative Therapeutic Solutions LLC, which provide comprehensive psychological/behavioral health services as well as training for clinicians and companies dedicated to empowering internal gifts, connecting thoughts with behaviors, developing character, and elevating mindsets. Check out his podcast, Black People Go to Therapy, on all platforms! His books, therapeutic tools, and contacts can be found @www.meetDrE.com, and he can be followed on social media @empowerallday.

References

Alcohol Health Res World. (1997) ;21(2):107-8. The principles of nerve cell communication.

Al-Hussaini A, Dorvlo AS, Antony SX, Chavan D, Dave J, Purecha V, Al-Rahbi S, Al-Adawi S. (2001). Vipassana meditation:: A naturalistic, preliminary observation in Muscat. J Sci Res Med Sci. 2001 Oct;3(2):87-92.

Anthony D., Dippe S., Hofeldt F., Davis J., Forsham P., (1973). Personality Disorder and Reactive Hypoglycemia: A Quantitative Study. Diabetes 1 September 1973; 22 (9): 664–675.

Badcock, P., (2019). "Explaining how the mind works A new theory," Research Outreach (110).

Bazira, P., (2021). An overview of the nervous system, Surgery (Oxford), Volume 39, Issue 8, Pages 451-462

Berkowitz, L. (1983). Aversively stimulated aggression: Some parallels and differences in research with animals and humans. American Psychologist, 38(11), 1135–1144.

Berkowitz L. (1990). On the formation and regulation of anger and aggression. A cognitive-neoassociationistic analysis. Am Psychol. Apr;45(4):494-503.

Berkowitz L. (2012). A different view of anger: the cognitive-neoassociation conception of the relation of anger to aggression. Aggress Behav. Jul-Aug;38(4):322-33.

Berkowitz L. (2000). Causes and Consequences of Feelings. Cambridge University Press.

Berkowitz, L., Cochran, S. T., & Embree, M. C. (1981). Physical pain and the goal of aversively stimulated aggression.

Journal of Personality and Social Psychology, 40(4), 687–700.

Billman GE. (2020). Homeostasis: The Underappreciated and Far Too Often Ignored Central Organizing Principle of Physiology. Front Physiol. 2020 Mar 10; 11:200.

Botvinick, M., Cohen, J. (1998). Rubber hands 'feel' touch that eyes see. Nature 391, 756.

Breit S, Kupferberg A, Rogler G, Hasler G. (2018). Vagus Nerve as Modulator of the Brain-Gut Axis in Psychiatric and Inflammatory Disorders. Front Psychiatry. Mar 13; 9:44.

Brinkman JE, Toro F, Sharma S. (2023). Physiology, Respiratory Drive. StatPearls. Treasure Island (FL): StatPearls Publishing.

A. Caplin, F.S. Chen, M.R. Beauchamp, E. Puterman, (2021). The effects of exercise intensity on the cortisol response to a subsequent acute psychosocial stressor, Psychoneuroendocrinology, Volume 131, 105336.

Charley E, Dinner B, Pham K, Vyas N. (2023). Diabetes as a consequence of acute pancreatitis. World J Gastroenterol. Aug 21;29(31):4736-4743.

Çiğdem Aksu, Duygu Ayar, (2023). The effects of visualization meditation on the depression, anxiety, stress, and achievement motivation levels of nursing students, Nurse Education Today, Volume 120, 2023, 105618.

Cohen, G. L., & Sherman, D. K. (2014). The psychology of change: Self-affirmation and social psychological intervention. Annual Review of Psychology, 65(1), 333–371.

Cross A, Sheffield D. (2016). Mental contrasting as a behaviour change technique: a systematic review protocol paper of effects, mediators, and moderators on health. Syst Rev. 2016 Nov 25;5(1):201.

Diamond A, (2012-2013). Executive functions. Annu Rev Psychol. 64:135-68. Epub Sep 27.

Dickerson, S. S., & Kemeny, M. E. (2004). Acute Stressors and Cortisol Responses: A Theoretical Integration and Synthesis of Laboratory Research. Psychological Bulletin, 130(3), 355–391.

Dirk De Ridder, Mark Llewellyn Smith, Divya Adhia, (2023). Chapter 4 - Autonomic nervous system and the triple network: an evolutionary perspective with clinical implications, Introduction to Quantitative EEG and Neurofeedback (Third Edition), Academic Press, Pages 63-77.

Drukarch B, Wilhelmus M, (2023). Thinking about the action potential: the nerve signal as a window to the physical principles guiding neuronal excitability. Frontiers in Cellular Neuroscience. Volume 17.

Dublin, J. E. (1976). "Beyond" Gestalt: Toward integrating some systems of psychotherapy. Psychotherapy: Theory, Research & Practice, 13(3), 225–231.

Ensari I., Schwartz J., Edmondson D., Duran A., Shimbo D., Diaz K., (2020). Testing the cross-stressor hypothesis under real-world conditions: exercise as a moderator of the association between momentary anxiety and cardiovascular responses. J Behav Med;43(6):989-1001.

Evans, R. (2021). *Run to the Pain.* Amazon KDP

Fadare, Stephen & Lambaco, Ermalyn & Mangorsi, Yasmin & Louise, Lorchano & Juvenmile, Tercio. (2022). A Voyage into the Visualization of Athletic Performances: A Review. American Journal of Multidisciplinary Research and Innovation. 1. 105-109.

Ferri, G., Cimini, G., (2020). Energy in Contemporary Reichian Analysis. International Body Psychotherapy Journal The Art and Science of Somatic Praxis Volume 19, Number 2, Fall/Winter 2020/2021, pp. 17-23.

Fuentes-García JP, Clemente-Suárez VJ, Marazuela-Martínez MÁ, Tornero-Aguilera JF, Villafaina S. (2021). Impact of Real and Simulated Flights on Psychophysiological Response of Military Pilots. Int J Environ Res Public Health. 2021 Jan 18;18(2):787.

Galli A, Ambrosini F, Lombardi F. (2016). Holter Monitoring and Loop Recorders: From Research to Clinical Practice. Arrhythm Electrophysiol Rev;5(2):136-43.

Gidon A, Aru J, Larkum ME (2022) Does brain activity cause consciousness? A thought experiment. PLOS Biology 20(6): e3001651.

Gillig PM. (2009). Dissociative identity disorder: a controversial diagnosis. Psychiatry (Edgmont). Mar;6(3):24-9.

Goleman, D. (1985), New York Times. New Focus on Multiple Personality, Section C. page 1.

Gollwitzer, P. M. (1999). Implementation intentions: Strong effects of simple plans. American Psychologist, 54(7), 493–503.

Gong W, Gu L, Wang W, Chen L, (2022). Interoception visualization relieves acute pain. Biol Psychol. 2022 Mar; 169:108276.

Hansen GH, Richardson DP, Li KM, Arnold JC, McGregor IS. (2009). Reintoxication: the release of fat-stored delta (9)-tetrahydrocannabinol (THC) into blood is enhanced by food deprivation or ACTH exposure. Br J Pharmacol. 2009 Nov;158(5):1330-7.

Hatton IA, Galbraith ED, Merleau NSC, Miettinen TP, Smith BM, Shander JA. (2023). The human cell count and size distribution. Proc Natl Acad Sci U S A. 2023 Sep 26;120(39).

Herculano-Houzel, S. (2009). The human brain in numbers: a linearly scaled-up primate brain. Frontiers in Human Neuroscience, Nov 9:3:31.

Heusch G, Thämer V. (1984) [Significance of the sympathetic nervous system for the coronary circulation]. Z Kardiol. 1984 Sep;73(9):543-51.

James, W. What is an emotion? Mind 1884, 34, 188–205.

J.B. Furness, (2009). Parasympathetic Nervous System, Editor(s): Larry R. Squire, Encyclopedia of Neuroscience, Academic Press, Pages 445-446.

Kahneman, D., & Tversky, A., (1979). "Prospect Theory: An Analysis of Decision Under Risk" published in Econometrica, volume 47, issue 2, pages 263-292.

Karemaker JM. (2017). An introduction into autonomic nervous function. Physiol Meas. 2017 May;38(5): R89-R118.

Kestly, T. A. (2016). Presence and play: Why mindfulness matters. International Journal of Play Therapy, 25(1), 14–23.

Klaperski S., Von Dawans B., Heinrichs M., Fuchs R. (2014). Effects of a 12-week endurance training program on the physiological response to psychosocial stress in men: a randomized controlled trial. J Behav Med. 37(6):1118-33.

Koukourikos K, Tsaloglidou A, Kourkouta L, Papathanasiou IV, Iliadis C, Fratzana A, Panagiotou A. (2021). Simulation in Clinical Nursing Education. Acta Inform Med. Mar;29(1):15-20.

Kuriyama A, Kasai H, Shikino K, Shiko Y, Kawame C, Takeda K, et al. (2023) The effects of simple graphical and mental visualization of lung sounds in teaching lung auscultation during clinical clerkship: A preliminary study.

Łakuta P. (2020). Using the theory of self-affirmation and self-regulation strategies of mental contrasting and forming implementation intentions to reduce social anxiety symptoms. Anxiety Stress Coping. 2020 Jul;33(4):370-386.

Lang PJ, Bradley MM. (2010). Emotion and the motivational brain. Biol Psychol. Jul;84(3):437-50.

Lebois L., Ross DA, Kaufman ML. (2022). "I Am Not I": The Neuroscience of Dissociative Identity Disorder. Biol Psychiatry. Feb 1;91(3): e11-e13.

Levenson RW, Ekman P, Ricard M. (2012). Meditation and the startle response: a case study. Emotion. Jun;12(3):650-8.

Levi, L. (1971). Society, Stress and Disease Vol. 1, the psychosocial environment and the psychosomatic disease. London: Oxford University.

Levine, H., (1997). Rest Heart Rate and Life Expectancy. Journal of the American College of Cardiology. Vol. 30(4):1104–1106.

Lin S., Cheng G., Sun S., Feng M., Bai X. (2024) Emotional Regulation of Displaced Aggression in Provocative Situations among Junior High School Students. Behav Sci (Basel). Jun 14;14(6):500.

Ludwig P., Reddy V., Varacallo M. (2023). Neuroanatomy, Neurons. StatPearls. Treasure Island (FL): StatPearls Publishing.

Osmo F., Duran V., Wenzel A., Reis de Oliveira I., Nepomuceno S., Madeira M., Menezes I. (2018). The Negative Core

Beliefs Inventory: Development and Psychometric Properties. J Cogn Psychother. Apr;32(1):67-84.

Max Baarspul, (1990). A review of flight simulation techniques, Progress in Aerospace Sciences, Volume 27, Issue 1, Pages 1-120.

McLean A., McDonald W., Goodridge D., (2020). Simulation Modeling as a Novel and Promising Strategy for Improving Success Rates With Research Funding Applications: A Constructive Thought Experiment JMIR Nursing;3(1): e18983.

McRae K., Gross JJ. (2020). Emotion regulation. Emotion. Feb;20(1):1-9.

McManus DE. (2017). Reiki Is Better Than Placebo and Has Broad Potential as a Complementary Health Therapy. J Evid Based Complementary Altern Med. Oct;22(4):1051-1057.

Messerli-Bürgy, N., Meyer, A., Kakebeeke, T., Stülb, K., Arhab, A., Zysset, A., Leeger-Aschmann, C., Schmutz, E., Thayer, J., Groene, M., Kriemler, S., Jenni, O., Puder, J., Munsch, S., (2020). Cardiac vagal tone in preschool children: Interrelations and the role of stress exposure, International Journal of Psychophysiology, Volume 152, Pages 102-109,

Mitrophanov AY, Groisman EA. (2008). Positive feedback in cellular control systems. Bioessays. Jun;30(6):542-55.

Modesti MN, Rapisarda L, Capriotti G, Del Casale A. (2022). Functional Neuroimaging in Dissociative Disorders: A Systematic Review. J Pers Med. Aug 29;12(9):1405.

Morris LS, McCall JG, Charney DS, Murrough JW. (2020). The role of the locus coeruleus in the generation of pathological anxiety. Brain Neurosci Adv. Jul 21;4.

Mostafa H., (2021). Different Cells of the Human Body: Categories and Morphological Characters. J Microsc Ultrastruct. Feb 16;10(2):40-46.

Newman T, (2023). All about the Nervous System. Medical News Today. https://www.medicalnewstoday.com/articles/307076.

Niveau, N., Beaudoin, M., & New, B. (2022). A new technique to increase self-esteem by reading and mental visualization: The lexical association technique. Journal of Social and Clinical Psychology, 41(1), 79–104.

Paul Rea, (2014). Introduction to the Nervous System, Editor(s): Paul Rea, Clinical Anatomy of the Cranial Nerves, Academic Press.

Perry, S., Khovanova, N.A. & Khovanov, I.A. (2019). Control of heart rate through guided high-rate breathing. Sci Rep 9, 1545.

Porges, S., (2004). Neuroception: A Subconscious System for Detecting Threats and Safety Zero to Three (J), v24 n5 p19-24 May 2004.

Prabu, P. K., & Subhash, J. (2015). Guided imagery therapy. Journal of Nursing and Health Science, 4(5), 56– 58.

Prochaska, James O.; DiClemente, Carlo C. (2005). "The transtheoretical approach.' In Norcross, John C.; Goldfried, Marvin R. (eds.). Handbook of psychotherapy integration. Oxford series in clinical psychology (2nd ed.). Oxford; New York: Oxford University Press. pp. 147– 171.

Prochaska JO, DiClemente CC, Norcross JC. (1992). In search of how people change. Applications to addictive behaviors. Am Psychol. Sep;47(9):1102-14.

Prochaska, James O.; Velicer, Wayne F. (1997). "The transtheoretical model of health behavior change" (PDF). American Journal of Health Promotion. 12 (1): 38–48.

Purves D, Augustine GJ, Fitzpatrick D, et al., (2001). Neuroscience. 2nd edition. Sunderland (MA): Sinauer Associates; How Ionic Movements Produce Electrical Signals.

Puterman, E., O'Donovan, A., Adler, N., Tomiyama, A., Kemeny, M., Wolkowitz, O., (2012). Physical activity moderates stressor-induced rumination on cortisol reactivity Psychosom. Med., 73 (2012), pp. 604-611.

Putnam F., Guroff J., Silberman E., Barban L., Post R. (1986). The clinical phenomenology of multiple personality disorder: review of 100 recent cases. J Clin Psychiatry. Jun;47(6):285-93.

Rafie, N., Kashou, A. H., & Noseworthy, P. A. (2021). ECG Interpretation: Clinical Relevance, Challenges, and Advances. Hearts, 2(4), 505-513.

Raihan N, Cogburn M., (2023). Stages of Change Theory. StatPearls [Internet]. Treasure Island (FL): StatPearls Publishing.

Ram D, Ashoka HG, Gowdappa B. (2015). Hyperglycemia associated dissociative fugue (organic dissociative disorder) in an elderly. J Family Med Prim Care. Jul-Sep;4(3):465-7.

Rassler B, Blinowska K, Kaminski M, Pfurtscheller G. (2023). Analysis of Respiratory Sinus Arrhythmia and Directed Information Flow between Brain and Body Indicate Different Management Strategies of fMRI-Related Anxiety. Biomedicines. Mar 27;11(4):1028.

Rasteiro A, Santos V, Massuça LM (2023). Physical Training Programs for Tactical Populations: Brief Systematic Review. Healthcare (Basel). Mar 28;11(7):967.

Rehan MA, Kuppa A, Ahuja A, Khalid S, Patel N, Budi Cardi FS, Joshi VV, Khalid A, Tohid H. (2018). A Strange Case of Dissociative Identity Disorder: Are There Any Triggers? Cureus. Jul 10;10(7).

Rimmele, U., Seiler, R., Marti, B., Wirtz, P., Ehlert, U., Heinrichs, M., (2009). The level of physical activity affects adrenal and cardiovascular reactivity to psychosocial stress Psychoneuroendocrinology, 34 (2009), pp. 190-198.

Rimmele, U., Zellweger, B., Marti, B., Seiler, R., Mohiyeddini, C., Ehlert, U., Heinrichs. M., (2007). Trained men show lower cortisol, heart rate and psychological responses to psychosocial stress compared with untrained men, Psychoneuroendocrinology, 32 (2007), pp. 627-635.

Sandy Fritz, Leon Chaitow, Glenn M. Hymel, (2008). Chapter 6 - Review of Pertinent Anatomy and Physiology, Editor(s): Sandy Fritz, Leon Chaitow, Glenn M. Hymel, Clinical Massage in the Healthcare Setting, Mosby, Pages 140-195.

Saxena M, Tote S, Sapkale B. (2023). Multiple Personality Disorder or Dissociative Identity Disorder: Etiology, Diagnosis, and Management. Cureus. Nov 19;15(11).

Schulz SM, Alpers GW, Hofmann SG. (2008). Negative self-focused cognitions mediate the effect of trait social anxiety on state anxiety. Behav Res Ther. 2008 Apr;46(4):438-49.

Scrimin, S., Patron, E., Peruzza, M., & Moscardino, U. (2020). Cardiac vagal tone and executive functions: Moderation by physical fitness and family support. Journal of Applied Developmental Psychology, 67, Article 101120.

Siehl, S., Zohair, R., Guldner, S., Nees, F., (2023). Gray matter differences in adults and children with posttraumatic stress disorder: A systematic review and meta-analysis of 113 studies and 11 meta-analyses, Journal of Affective Disorders, Volume 333, Pages 489-516.

Strachan, S., Myre, M., Berry, T., Ceccarelli, L., Semenchuk, B., Miller, C., (2020). Self-affirmation and physical activity messages, Psychology of Sport and Exercise, Volume 47, 101613.

Sharkey, Keith, Mawe & Gary, (2023). The enteric nervous system. Physiological Reviews, p 1487-1564, V103:2.

Šimić, G., Tkalčić, M., Vukić, V., Mulc, D., Španić, E., Šagud, M., Olucha-Bordonau, F., Vukšić, M., R. Hof, P., (2021). Understanding Emotions: Origins and Roles of the Amygdala. Biomolecules, 11, 823.

Smallwood J., Turnbull A., Wang H., Ho N., Poerio G., Karapanagiotidis T., Konu D., Mckeown B., Zhang M., Murphy C., Vatansever D., Bzdok D., Konishi M., Leech R., Seli P., Schooler J., Bernhardt B., Margulies D., Jefferies E., (2021). The neural correlates of ongoing conscious thought. iScience. Feb 1;24(3):102132.

Sothmann M., Buckworth J., Claytor R., Cox R., White-Welkley J., Dishman R. (1996). Exercise training and the cross-stressor adaptation hypothesis. Exerc Sport Sci Rev; 24:267-87.

Stergiou M., Robles-Pérez J., Rey-Mota J., Tornero-Aguilera J., Clemente-Suárez V., (2023). Psychophysiological Responses in Soldiers during Close Combat: Implications for Occupational Health and Fitness in Tactical Populations. Healthcare (Basel). 2023 Dec 29;12(1):82.

Stone, D. (2008). Wounded healing: Exploring the circle of compassion in the helping relationship. The Humanistic Psychologist, 36(1), 45–51.

Stranahan A., Lee K., & Mattson M., (2008). Central mechanisms of HPA axis regulation by voluntary exercise. Neuromolecular Med. 2008;10(2):118-27.

Strasburger, H. & Waldvogel, B. (2015), Sight and blindness in the same person. PsyCh Journal, 4: 178-185.

Sun J., He L., Chen Q., Yang W., Wei D., Qiu J., (2022). The bright side and dark side of daydreaming predict creativity together through brain functional connectivity. Hum Brain Mapp. 2022 Feb 15;43(3):902-914.

Szabo, S., Tache, Y., & Somogyi, A. (2012). The legacy of Hans Selye and the origins of stress research: A retrospective 75 years after his landmark brief "Letter" to the Editor# of Nature. Stress, 15(5), 472–478.

Tan SY, Yip A. (2018) Hans Selye (1907-1982): Founder of the stress theory. Singapore Med J. 2018 Apr;59(4):170-171.

Thayer J, Lane R., (2007). The role of vagal function in the risk for cardiovascular disease and mortality. Biol Psychol. Feb;74(2):224-42.

Traustadóttir, T., Bosch, P., Matt, K., (2005). The HPA axis response to stress in women: effects of aging and fitness Psychoneuroendocrinology, 30 (2005), pp. 392-402.

Vilensky, J., (2014). The neglected cranial nerve: nervus terminalis (cranial nerve N). Clinical Anatomy, 27(1), 46-53.

Von Dawans, B., Kirschbaum, C., & Heinrichs, M. (2011). The Trier Social Stress Test for Groups (TSST-G): A new research tool for controlled simultaneous social stress exposure in a group format. PNEC, 36, 514–522.

Wang X., Nawaz M., DuPont C., Myers J., Burke S., Bannister R., Foy B., Voss A., Rich M. (2022). The role of action potential changes in depolarization-induced failure of excitation contraction coupling in mouse skeletal muscle. Elife. 2022 Jan 5;11: e71588. doi: 10.7554/eLife.71588. PMID: 34985413; PMCID: PMC8730720.

Wang Y., Vlemincx E., Vantieghem I., Dhar M., Dong D., Vandekerckhove M. (2022). Bottom-Up and Cognitive Top-Down Emotion Regulation: Experiential Emotion Regulation and Cognitive Reappraisal on Stress Relief and Follow-Up Sleep Physiology. Int J Environ Res Public Health. 2022 Jun 22;19(13):7621.

Wang G., Wang Y., Gai X., (2021). A Meta-Analysis of the Effects of Mental Contrasting With Implementation Intentions on Goal Attainment. Frontiers in Psychology, Volume 12.

Levi L. 1971. Society, Stress and disease, Vol. 1, The psychosocial environment and psychosomatic disease. London: Oxford University Press.

Waxenbaum JA, Reddy V, Varacallo MA. (2023). Anatomy, Autonomic Nervous System. StatPearls. Treasure Island (FL): StatPearls Publishing

Wunsch, K., Wurst, R., Von Dawans, B., Strahler, J., Kasten, N., Fuchs, R., (2019). Habitual and acute exercise effects on salivary biomarkers in response to psychosocial stress Psychoneuroendocrinology, 106 (2019), pp. 216-225,

Yao M, Zhou Y, Li J, Gao X. (2019). Violent video games exposure and aggression: The role of moral disengagement, anger, hostility, and disinhibition. Aggress Behav. 2019 Nov;45(6):662-670.

Yaribeygi H, Panahi Y, Sahraei H, Johnston TP, Sahebkar A. (2017). The impact of stress on body function: A review. EXCLI J. 2017 Jul 21; 16:1057-1072.

Zhang GQ, Zhang W. (2009). Heart rate, lifespan, and mortality risk. Ageing Res Rev. Jan;8(1):52-60.

www.ingramcontent.com/pod-product-compliance
Lightning Source LLC
Chambersburg PA
CBHW042320090526
44585CB00024BA/2661